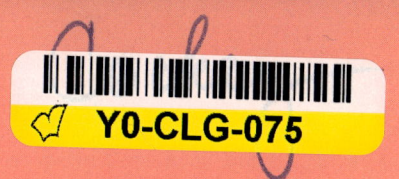

MEALS
with a
FOREIGN FLAIR

Better Homes and Gardens

MEREDITH PRESS

BETTER HOMES AND GARDENS CREATIVE COOKING LIBRARY, THIRD PRINTING
©MEREDITH PUBLISHING COMPANY, 1963. ALL RIGHTS RESERVED
PRINTED IN THE UNITED STATES OF AMERICA

Contents

For fabulous parties— foreign meals 6

    Sumptuous smörgåsbord
    Vive la cuisine française!
    Down Mexico way
    Specialties from sunny Spain
    In the Italian manner
    Salute to the Swiss
    Stout-hearted German fare
    Russian spectacular
    Honorable Chinese dinner

Around the world— a la carte 28

    Appetizers and snacks
    Meats and main dishes
    Wonderful with cheese
    Rice, vegetables, salads
    Breads from abroad
    Dramatic desserts

This seal means recipe goodness!

Every recipe in this book is *endorsed* by Better Homes & Gardens Test Kitchen. Each food was tested over and over till it rated superior — in practicality, ease of preparation, and deliciousness.

← Here's dinnertime drama a la Old Mexico. The star—zingy Enchiladas. Tickets to a bull fight afterward?

All aboard! With a cook book as a passport, let's travel 'round the world!

Smörgåsbord means fine food—in abundance. Here are Scandinavian inspirations, yours to borrow—fish delights, meat balls, brown beans, fruit desserts and fine cheese, fragile cookies. Serve with pride!

For fabulous parties... foreign meals

Scandinavia's favorite—sumptuous smörgåsbord!

Sweden, Denmark, and Norway have all contributed to the friendly smörgåsbord, making it rich in tradition and a culinary delight. We give a Swedish version:

Plan plenty of table room—extend your dining table or line up card tables. Wrap a drawer in a sheet, invert in center of table (to divide it in traditional thirds). Cover all with large cloth, or felt and tarlatan. Add Scandinavian trims, if you have them, and pretty candles, napkin fans.

Guests come to smörgåsbord three times —for appetizers, meats, desserts. (Clean plates each time!) Now—the recipes!

Smörgåsbord

Egg-and-Olive Penguins
Anchovy Stuffed Eggs
Herring Salad   Pickled Herring
Anchovies   Smoked Salmon
Sardines   Pickled Beets
Pickled Shrimp   Sliced Liver Pate
Stuffed Celery   Potatoes with Dill
Swedish Breads

• • •

Swedish Meat Balls* Brown Beans*
Fish Balls (*not shown*)
Decorated Chilled Ham
Vegetable Salad Cups
Red-and-white Salad

• • •

Fruit Compote
Lingonberry Sauce*
Danish Cheeses   Crackers
Scandinavian Cookies
Swedish Coffee

*See index for recipe

Egg-and-Olive Penguins

Each little fellow is fashioned from a big hard-cooked egg, a couple of "giant" ripe olives and a few pieces of carrot.

Cut thin slice from large end of each peeled egg, stand up. For penguin's head, peg olive to egg with toothpick. Use ¼ of a ripe olive (cut lengthwise) for each wing, a lengthwise sliver for the "necktie"; toothpick in place.

For feet, cut a lengthwise slice of carrot, a little less than ⅛ inch thick; cut the slice crosswise in ¾-inch lengths. Taper sides of each piece of carrot and notch wide end to make webbed foot; tuck a pair part way under each egg. Whittle a beak from carrot and push into "head."

Anchovy Stuffed Eggs

6 hard-cooked eggs, cut in half lengthwise
¼ cup mayonnaise
Dash pepper
1 to 2 tablespoons finely cut canned anchovy fillets

Remove egg yolks; mash. Blend in mayonnaise and pepper. Stir in anchovies to taste. Fill whites with mixture, using pastry tube if desired. (For that brimful look of plenty, fill only 8 of the whites; chop extras for a salad garnish.) Chill. Trim with diced pimiento, bits of parsley.

Stuffed Celery

Stuff celery with mixture of cream cheese and crumbled blue cheese (add to suit your taste) beaten together until fluffy. Dot filled stalks with capers and tiny pimiento diamonds.

To serve, stand stalks up around inverted tumbler. Hide glass with celery leaves.

First stop—appetizer table. Remember, this is only the start!

Trio of Egg-and-Olive Penguins guards the Anchovy Stuffed Eggs. Bedded on ice on the Lazy Susan: Herring Salad, pickled herring, rolled anchovies, sardines with pert lemon-slice trim, smoked salmon, and pickled beets.

Still room on your plate? Try sliced liver pate, (trimmed with chopped aspic), Pickled Shrimp, and Stuffed Celery (propped tall against glass).

Go-withs include boiled potatoes with dill (in the chafing dish) and a basketful of dark delicious Swedish breads.

Herring Salad (*Sillsallad*)

1½ pounds salt herring

· · ·

2 pared medium potatoes, cooked and finely cubed
4 medium beets, cooked, peeled, and finely cubed or cut in julienne strips
1 medium apple, pared and finely cubed
1 tablespoon finely chopped Bermuda onions
2 medium-size sweet pickles, finely cubed
1 tablespoon sugar
2 tablespoons vinegar
¼ teaspoon white pepper

· · ·

½ cup whipping cream, whipped (*optional*)

Soak herring overnight in water to cover. Bone; skin, and cut in small cubes.

Lightly mix herring, potatoes, beets, apple, onion, pickles, sugar, vinegar, and pepper. Chill. Fold in whipped cream just before serving.*

Serve on appetizer tray. Garnish with sieved hard-cooked egg yolks and finely chopped hard-cooked egg whites. Makes about 6 cups of Herring Salad.

*Or fold whipped cream in with other ingredients and mold in loaf pan.

Pickled Shrimp

2 to 2½ pounds fresh or frozen shrimp in shells
½ cup celery tops
¼ cup mixed pickling spices
1 tablespoon salt

· · ·

2 cups sliced onions
7 or 8 bay leaves

· · ·

Pickling Marinade:
1½ cups salad oil
¾ cup white vinegar
3 tablespoons capers and juice
2½ teaspoons celery seed
1½ teaspoons salt
Few drops bottled hot pepper sauce

Cover shrimp with boiling water; add celery tops, pickling spices, and salt. Cover and simmer for 5 minutes. Drain, then peel and devein under cold water. Alternate cleaned shrimp, onions, and bay leaves in shallow baking dish.

Combine remaining ingredients for Pickling Marinade. Mix well. Pour over shrimp.

Cover; chill at least 24 hours, spooning marinade over shrimp occasionally. Drain, remove bay leaves. Serve shrimp and onion slices on relish tray; or perch shrimp on glass rim; fill glass with onion slices. (Pickled Shrimp will keep at least a week in refrigerator.) Makes 6 servings.

Return to table for hot delicacies, meats, pretty chilled salads

It's time for fresh plates, so flavors from the three parts of the meal won't mingle. (Paper plates are dandy!)

Guests help themselves to tiny Swedish Meat Balls and Brown Beans, kept *hot* over the candle warmers.

For contrast—*chilled* ham, and Vegetable Salad Cups—a mixture of peas, carrots, and asparagus in mayonnaise. Sample Red-and-white Salad with this course, too.

A smörgåsbord lends itself to holiday entertaining—here all decked out for Christmas.

Decorated Chilled Ham

A triangle of bread, covered with salad greens, makes the backdrop; radishes, red apple are accents. Glamour for a few pennies!—

Place a chilled canned ham on large platter. For cucumber-slice trim, run tines of a fork down on unpared cucumber, notching the skin all around. Cut cucumber in ¼-inch slices, then cut slices in half. Stand these half-circles on edge, overlapping them, to make 2 parallel rows along top of ham at side edges.

Between cucumber rows center a bundle of 3 or 4 chilled canned asparagus spears; "tie" with strip of pimiento.

For a Yuletide touch, wrap an asparagus spear in a thin ham slice and stand it on end to resemble a candle at center of one side of ham; toothpick in place. Repeat same decoration on other side.

For the dramatic backdrop, stand a big wedge of bread (about ⅓ of an unsliced loaf) on its smallest side with the long slope toward one end of the ham. Completely cover bread with lettuce and curly endive, tacking with toothpicks; dot with radish roses (also held by toothpicks).

For a touch of color nestle a bright red apple between greenery and ham. Garnish platter with lettuce or individual vegetable salads, as shown.

Red-and-white Salad

Make 1 recipe each Red Tomato Mold and Snowy Cheese Mold. Unmold both salads; cut in wide slices. Alternate them, red and white, reassembling in two identical salads. (See picture, page 7.)

Tuck in greens for trim. Recipe makes two salads, or 12 servings.

Red Tomato Mold

    4 cups tomato juice
    ⅓ cup chopped onion
    ¼ cup chopped celery leaves
    2 tablespoons brown sugar
    1 teaspoon salt
    2 small bay leaves
    4 whole cloves

    . . .

    2 envelopes (2 tablespoons) unflavored gelatin
    3 tablespoons lemon juice

Combine *2 cups* of the tomato juice, the onion, celery leaves, sugar, salt, bay leaves, and cloves. Simmer uncovered 5 minutes. Strain.

Meanwhile, soften gelatin in *1 cup* of the remaining *cold* tomato juice; dissolve in *hot* tomato mixture. Add remaining tomato juice and the lemon juice. Pour into a 5-cup ring mold; chill till firm.

Smörgåsbord

Snowy Cheese Mold

1 12-ounce carton (1½ cups)
  cream-style cottage cheese
2 3-ounce packages cream cheese,
  softened
½ cup finely chopped celery
2 tablespoons finely chopped chives
¼ teaspoon salt
1 envelope (1 tablespoon)
  unflavored gelatin
¼ cup cold water

. . .

1 cup mayonnaise

With electric or rotary beater, beat together cottage cheese and cream cheese till fluffy. Stir in celery, chives, and salt. Soften gelatin in cold water; dissolve over hot water. Stir into cheese mixture. Stir in mayonnaise. Pour into a 5-cup ring mold. Chill till firm. Makes 6 servings.

Bowknots (Fattigmann)

Tender cookies, light as feathers. Your deep-fat fryer does the cooking—

6 egg yolks
¼ cup sugar
1 tablespoon melted butter or
  margarine
⅛ cup whipping cream, whipped
1 teaspoon ground cardamom
2 cups sifted all-purpose flour
½ teaspoon salt

Beat the egg yolks until thick and lemon-colored; gradually beat in sugar. Gently stir in butter. Fold in whipped cream and cardamom. Sift together flour and salt; gradually fold into yolk mixture just enough to make soft dough. Chill well. Divide dough in half. On lightly floured surface, roll each piece to ⅛ inch. Cut in 3x¾-inch strips.* Cut a slit lengthwise in center of each and pull one end through. Fry a few at a time in deep, hot fat (375°) about 1 to 1½ minutes, or till a very light golden brown. Drain on paper towels. While warm, sift a little confectioners' sugar over. Makes about 5 dozen.

*For Bowknots with points at ends, cut dough in long strips, 2 inches wide, then slash diagonally at 3-inch lengths to make diamonds. Cut slit in center as above.

Cooky Tarts (Sandbakelser)

Thoroughly cream 1 cup *each* butter and sugar; add 1 egg and beat well. Add 1 teaspoon almond extract. Stir in 3 cups sifted all-purpose flour. Pinch off small ball of dough and place in center of sandbakelse mold (or use tiny foilware pans); with thumb, press evenly and very thinly over bottom and sides. Place molds on cooky sheet. Bake at 350° about 12 minutes. Cool.

Invert molds; tap lightly. (Clean molds with dry cloth.) Fill cookies with jam or whipped cream. Makes 5 dozen.

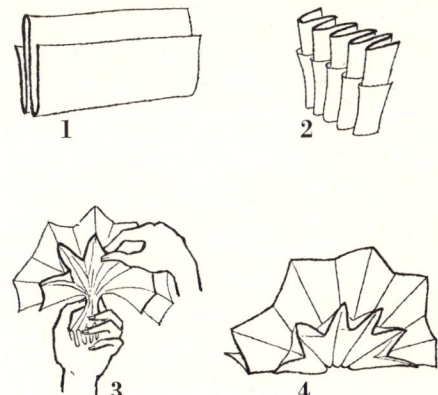

Napkin Fans

Choose square napkins with some body, or starch lightly. (Ours were 17 inches square).

Following diagram No. 1, above, fold napkin in half; then fold each side ⅔ of distance back toward center fold. Press.

Fold in accordion pleats, (No. 2), each about 1½ inches wide—a little wider if napkins are larger than ours. Crease.

Following diagram No. 3, grasp napkin at bottom so it unfolds like a fan. Make small inverted pleats between the larger pleats: Pull forward and down on the top of each *inside* fold of the *shorter* piece in front, till it lines up with the outside folds. Crease tightly with fingers to make sharp edge. Repeat on other side of napkin. Fold napkin fans closed and place under heavy object for several hours.

When you set the table, open the fan, letting flat ends make the base (No. 4).

Vive la cuisine française!

Bon Appétit!

Salade Jardinière
Fish with Tarragon Butter
Duckling with Orange Sauce
French Fries
(*Pommes de Terre Frites*)
Green Salad   Brioche
French Strawberry Tart
Demitasse

Salade Jardinière

Each guest rates an individual appetizer: On salad plate, group chilled marinated green beans, tiny pickled beets, shredded carrot sprinkled with sugar and vinegar, and egg slices with mustard-mayonnaise. Trim with tender water-cress sprigs.

Fish with Tarragon Butter
(*Poisson au Beurre d'Estragon*)

Thaw 1 pound frozen fish fillets. Cut in 4 pieces. Salt and pepper. Place on greased broiler pan. Spread with Tarragon Butter; broil 4 inches from heat about 4 to 5 minutes. Serve as second course of meal, passing extra Butter. Serves 4.

Tarragon Butter: Cream ¼ cup butter till fluffy; blend in ½ teaspoon dried tarragon and 1 teaspoon lemon juice. Let stand an hour at room temperature.

Green Salad (*Salade Verte*)

For drama, fix French salad at the table! Rub salad bowl with cut clove of garlic. Measure in ½ teaspoon salt, ¼ teaspoon dry mustard, and ¼ teaspoon paprika; blend. With fork, beat in ¼ cup salad oil.

Add 4 cups chilled dry greens (any combination). Toss lightly till leaves glisten. Sprinkle with 2 tablespoons *each* vinegar and lemon juice; toss. Serves 6.

Duckling with Orange Sauce
(*Caneton à l'Orange*)

Purchase 4- to 5-pound ready-to-cook duckling. Remove wing joints and tips, leaving only meaty second joints. Rub duckling inside with salt and pepper. Skewer opening, lace. Place breast up on rack in roasting pan. Do not add water.

Roast at 425° for 15 minutes; turn oven down to 350° and continue roasting 1 hour and 40 minutes, or till done, spooning off fat occasionally. Duck is done when meaty part of leg feels tender (use paper towel). Meanwhile, begin Orange Sauce.

When duck is done, tip slightly so inside juices drain into roasting pan. Remove skewers; place bird on hot platter. Sprinkle lightly with salt, and keep warm.

Finish Orange Sauce. Spoon part over duck; pass remainder. Garnish bird with a row of orange sections. Makes 4 servings.

Orange Sauce

2 medium oranges
½ cup sugar
1 tablespoon red wine vinegar
¼ cup orange liqueur
Juices from roast duck

Grate peel from *one* orange (2 teaspoons). With vegetable parer, shave peel from other orange in long thin strips (¼ cup). Squeeze juice from oranges (⅔ cup).

In heavy skillet, cook and stir sugar and vinegar just till sugar caramelizes to a rich brown. At once remove from heat; add *grated* orange peel, orange juice, and liqueur. Return to heat and simmer, stirring till caramelized sugar dissolves.

After transferring roast duck to a platter, skim off fat from juices in roasting pan. Add orange-juice mixture to juices in pan. Cook, stirring constantly and scraping sides of pan, for a few minutes or till of desired sauce consistency. Stir in the *strips* of peel. Squeeze in a little lemon juice. Spoon part of sauce over duckling; pass remainder.

French Strawberry Tart
(Tarte aux Fraises)

    2 8-ounce packages cream cheese, softened
    ¼ cup sugar
    1 to 2 teaspoons grated lemon peel
    2 tablespoons lemon juice
    1 baked 9-inch Rich Tart Shell
    1 quart fresh strawberries, sliced
    2 tablespoons cornstarch
    ¼ cup cold water
    1 12-ounce jar (1 cup) strawberry preserves
    2 tablespoons lemon juice

Combine first 4 ingredients; mix well. Spread in baked shell. Top with berries.

Combine cornstarch and water; add preserves. Bring to boiling, stirring constantly; cook and stir until thick and clear. Remove from heat; add 2 tablespoons lemon juice. Cool to room temperature. Pour over berries. Chill. Makes 12 servings.

Rich Tart Shell

Stir ½ cup butter to soften; blend in ¼ cup sugar and ¼ teaspoon salt. Add 1 egg; mix well. Stir in 1½ cups sifted all-purpose flour. Chill slightly.

On floured surface, roll out in 12-inch circle. Using rolling pin to transfer dough, carefully place over *outside* of 9-inch round cake pan. (Shape dough to sides of pan *almost* to rim. Be sure there are *no thin places*, especially at corner.) Trim.

Place pan, crust up, on cooky sheet. Bake at 450° for 8 to 10 minutes or till lightly browned. Cool few minutes; while slightly warm, transfer crust to plate.

Demitasse

In coffee server, mix 3 tablespoons instant coffee and 2 cups boiling water. Serve in small cups, usually black, with or without sugar. (Or pass whipped cream.) Makes 6 ⅓-cup servings.

It's good! A French Strawberry Tart is a show-off for luscious berries—

down Mexico way

After a Mexican meal—break a Pinata! Make a gay papier-mache parrot (*below*); cut a small hole in back; fill with favors, and hang from ceiling. Blindfold guests and let them bat away—for fun and surprises!

Pinata Party

Guacamole*   Tostadas*
Enchiladas
Tamales
Crisp Green Salad
Caramel Puddings
Panocha   Limeade

*See index listing

Caramel Puddings

Make caramel syrup: melt ¼ cup sugar in heavy skillet, stirring till rich brown. Remove from heat. Slowly add ½ cup boiling water. Return to heat; stir till smooth.

Combine ¼ cup sugar, 3 tablespoons cornstarch, and ¼ teaspoon salt in saucepan; blend in 2 cups milk. Stir in caramel syrup. Cook and stir over medium heat till thick. Cook 2 minutes more. Add 1½ teaspoons vanilla. Pour into bowls. Add Caramel Trim. Chill. Serves 5 or 6.

Caramel Trim: Melt ½ cup sugar in heavy skillet over low heat, stirring constantly. When golden, remove from heat, immediately drizzle over puddings. The syrup hardens to crackly "candy."

Enchiladas

1½ cups chopped onion
Olive oil
2 1-pound cans (4 cups) tomatoes
2 8-ounce cans seasoned tomato sauce
2 cloves garlic, minced
2 to 3 teaspoons finely chopped canned green chiles
1 tablespoon chili powder
2 teaspoons sugar
1 teaspoon salt
¾ pound ground beef
1 small clove garlic, minced
½ cup sliced green onion
3 tablespoons chopped ripe olives
2 teaspoons chili powder
¾ teaspoon salt
Puffy Tortillas*
1½ cups shredded sharp process cheese
Ripe olives, sliced lengthwise

Make sauce: Cook chopped onion in 2 tablespoons olive oil till tender. Add next 7 ingredients; simmer uncovered 30 minutes.

Make enchiladas: For filling, cook beef and garlic in 1 tablespoon olive oil, add next 4 ingredients. Prepare Puffy Tortillas*; fill with 2 to 3 tablespoons filling, 1 tablespoon cheese; roll up. (Enchiladas and sauce can be made ahead, chilled. Combine; bake at 350° about 1 hour.)

To serve: Arrange enchiladas in sauce on heatproof platter; sprinkle with remaining cheese, olives. Bake at 350° about 25 minutes. Makes 6 servings.

Puffy Tortillas: Sift together ¾ cup sifted all-purpose flour, ¾ cup yellow corn meal, and ¼ teaspoon salt; add 1 beaten egg, and 1¾ cups water; beat smooth. Pour 3 tablespoons batter in hot greased 6-inch skillet; cook till brown on bottom and top is just set (2 to 3 minutes). Loosen with spatula, flip out on paper towel.

*Or use frozen tortillas. Fry as directed; then heat in sauce. Fill immediately!

For fun, make your own Pinata!

Cover 2 balloons and shape wings, beak, using paste-soaked paper strips. Dry overnight. Deflate, remove balloons. Tape parts together. Fringe 3-inch-wide lengthwise folds of tissue paper, turn inside out; paste on pinata, overlapping strips.

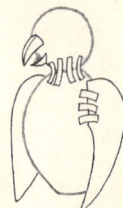

Specialties from sunny Spain

Spanish Fiesta

Gazpacho with Croutons
Spanish Olives
Paella
Escarole with
Vinegar-Oil Dressing
Banana-Nut Cake   Coffee

Gazpacho

1 cup finely chopped peeled tomato
½ cup *each* finely chopped green pepper, celery, and cucumber
¼ cup finely chopped onion
2 teaspoons snipped parsley
1 teaspoon snipped chives
1 small clove garlic, minced
2 to 3 tablespoons tarragon wine vinegar
2 tablespoons olive oil
1 teaspoon salt
¼ teaspoon black pepper
½ teaspoon Worcestershire sauce
2 cups tomato juice

Combine ingredients in stainless-steel or glass bowl. Cover; chill at least 4 hours. Serve in chilled cups. Pass crisp Croutons. Makes 6 servings.

Croutons: Cut slightly dry bread in ½-inch cubes. Melt a little butter in a skillet; add bread cubes; toss lightly. Heat and stir till croutons are golden brown.

Spanish Paella (*pah-ehl-yeh*)

1 3-pound ready-to-eat chicken, cut up
5 cups water
2 carrots, sliced lengthwise
2 onions, quartered
1 celery stalk with leaves
2½ to 3 teaspoons salt
¼ teaspoon coarse black pepper
⅔ cup long-grain rice
2 cloves garlic, crushed
¼ cup olive oil
¼ cup diced pimiento
½ teaspoon oregano
¼ teaspoon Spanish saffron
1 package frozen artichoke hearts, thawed enough to separate
⅔ pound shelled raw shrimp (1 pound in shell)
1 10½-ounce can clams

Place chicken in Dutch oven; add next 6 ingredients. Bring to boil, reduce heat, cover; simmer 1 hour or till just tender. Remove chicken; bone, cut up meat. Strain stock; save 4 cups. Fry rice and garlic in olive oil over medium heat, stirring constantly till rice is browned, about 10 minutes. Add reserved stock, pimiento, oregano, and saffron. Cover, cook over low heat 15 minutes. Add chicken and last 3 ingredients. Bring to boil, cover, cook over very low heat 15 minutes. Serves 6.

Banana-Nut Cake

Stir ⅔ cup shortening to soften. Sift in 2½ cups sifted cake flour, 1⅔ cups sugar, 1¼ teaspoons baking powder, 1 teaspoon soda, and 1 teaspoon salt. Add 1¼ cups mashed fully ripe bananas and ⅓ cup buttermilk; mix till flour is dampened. Beat vigorously 2 minutes. Add ⅓ cup buttermilk and 2 eggs; beat 2 minutes. Fold in ⅔ cup chopped walnuts.

Bake in 2 paper-lined 9-inch round pans in moderate oven (350°) about 35 minutes. Cool 10 minutes in pans; remove; cool. Frost with Panocha Frosting.

Panocha Frosting: Melt ½ cup butter; add 1 cup brown sugar. Bring to boiling; cook and stir 1 minute or until slightly thickened. Cool 15 minutes. Add ¼ cup hot milk; beat until smooth. Beat in sifted confectioners' sugar till frosting is of spreading consistency (takes about 3¼ cups). Frosts two 9-inch layers.

In the Italian manner

Heat oil in large skillet till hot enough to sizzle drop of water; add chicken and brown slowly turning once with tongs. Remove chicken; cook onions and garlic in the oil.

....

As the Romans Do!

Antipasto
Chicken Cacciatora
Buttered Noodles with Parmesan
Romaine with Hot Italian Dressing
Tutti-frutti Tortoni
Cappuccino

....

Chicken Cacciatora
(*Pollo alla Cacciatora*)

¼ cup olive oil
1 2½- to 3-pound ready-to-cook broiler-fryer chicken, cut up
2 medium onions, cut in ¼-inch slices
2 cloves garlic, minced
1 1-pound can (2 cups) tomatoes
1 8-ounce can seasoned tomato sauce
1 teaspoon salt
¼ teaspoon pepper
½ teaspoon celery seed
1 teaspoon crushed oregano or basil
1 or 2 bay leaves
¼ cup cooking sauterne

Heat olive oil in skillet; add chicken pieces; brown slowly, turning once. Remove chicken from skillet; cook onions and garlic in oil till tender, but not brown. Combine remaining ingredients, except cooking wine. Return chicken to skillet, add sauce mixture. Cover and simmer 45 minutes. Stir in cooking wine.

Cook uncovered, turning occasionally, 20 minutes or till fork-tender. Remove bay leaves; skim off excess fat. Serve chicken with sauce ladled over. Makes 4 servings.

Return chicken to skillet; add sauce. Cover, simmer 45 minutes—but don't bubble hard. Add cooking wine, cook uncovered till chicken is tender and sauce resembles chili sauce.

Discard bay leaves and skim off excess fat. Serve chicken with well-buttered noodles, or spaghetti sprinkled with Parmesan. Trim with gay, zesty Italian pickled peppers.

Italy

Zesty starter—Antipasto! Any combo of Italian relishes goes. We show Marinated Artichoke Hearts, a variety of peppers (mild, sweet and pickled), olives, sliced pepperoni, and salami roll-ups.

Marinated Artichoke Hearts

Cook a package of frozen artichoke hearts according to package directions; drain. Pour Hot Italian Dressing over and chill several hours, spooning dressing over a few times. Drain; serve on antipasto tray.

Hot Italian Dressing

1 teaspoon salt
½ teaspoon white pepper
¼ teaspoon cayenne
¼ teaspoon dry mustard
3 tablespoons salad vinegar
1 tablespoon lemon juice
1 cup salad oil
3 cloves garlic, minced
Dash bottled hot pepper sauce

Combine ingredients; cover, shake vigorously. Serve over salad of romaine, thin-sliced red onions, and crisp croutons. *Or* use as marinade for artichoke hearts. Makes 1¼ cups dressing.

Tutti-frutti Tortoni

Stir 1 pint vanilla ice cream to soften. Add ¼ cup chopped candied fruits and peels, ¼ cup chopped seedless raisins, and rum flavoring to taste. Spoon into 4 or 5 paper bake cups set in muffin pan. Freeze till nearly firm, poke in whole toasted almonds, point down, and freeze firm.

Cappuccino

¼ cup instant espresso or instant dark-roast coffee
2 cups boiling water
½ cup whipping cream, whipped
Cinnamon, nutmeg, or finely shredded orange peel

Dissolve coffee in water. Pour into small cups, filling about half full. Offer sugar. Pass whipped cream—each adds a dollop, dashes it lightly with cinnamon, nutmeg, or orange peel, then folds in cream till frothy. Makes 6 or 7 servings.

Salute to the Swiss

Amid Alpine peaks and picturesque villages, the Swiss turn out some of the world's finest cheeses, chocolates, and fondues.

What better finale to an afternoon of skiing, ice-skating, or tobogganing than a cook-it-yourself fondue supper? You could almost imagine yourself in a Swiss chalet!

Chalet Special

Onion-Bibb Salad
Beef Fondue with Sauces
Ripe Pears and Green Grapes
Swiss Cheese
Dessert Pancakes
Whipped Orange Butter
Cinnamon Honey
Coffee
Swiss Chocolate

Onion-Bibb Salad

- 4 heads Bibb lettuce, separated in leaves
- 2 cups (1 bunch) water cress, with stems cut short
- ¾ cup very-thin-sliced mild onion, separated in rings
- 1 cup sliced unpared cucumber, (optional)
- 2 tablespoons salad oil
- 1 tablespoon tarragon vinegar
- ½ teaspoon Worcestershire sauce
- ¾ teaspoon salt
- ¼ teaspoon sugar
- Fresh-ground coarse black pepper

Place chilled dry greens, onion, and cucumber in salad bowl. Zigzag stream of salad oil over, then a mixture of the vinegar and Worcestershire. Sprinkle with salt and sugar. Grind pepper over *generously*. Toss gently. Makes 6 servings.

Beef Fondue

- Salad oil for cooking
- 1½ pounds trimmed beef tenderloin, cut in ¾-inch cubes
- Garlic Butter
- Anchovy Butter
- Caper Sauce
- Tomato Steak Sauce
- Horseradish Cream

Pour salad oil in a beef-fondue cooker or *deep* chafing dish* to depth of about 1½ inches. Place on range; bring to 425°. Take to table; place over alcohol burner or canned heat. Have beef cubes at room temperature in serving bowl. Set out small bowls of several or all of the special butters and sauces. Each guest spears a beef cube with fork, holds it in the hot oil until cooked to desired doneness, then dips it in a sauce on his plate.

When salad oil cools so meat no longer cooks briskly, heat oil again on range.

*An electric saucepan is ideal—it's deep, will heat oil and keep it hot.

Garlic Butter

Whip ½ cup soft butter and 1 clove minced garlic till fluffy.

Anchovy Butter

- 1 2-ounce can anchovy fillets
- ½ cup butter, softened
- 2 tablespoons olive oil
- ½ teaspoon paprika
- ⅛ teaspoon freshly ground pepper

Drain anchovies; place in mixer bowl with remaining ingredients; beat smooth.

Caper Sauce

Dry ¼ cup drained chopped sour pickle and 2 tablespoons drained finely chopped capers on paper towels. Add to 1 cup mayonnaise. Stir in 1½ teaspoons *each* prepared mustard and snipped parsley.

Switzerland

Tomato Steak Sauce

1 8-ounce can seasoned tomato sauce
⅓ cup bottled steak sauce
2 tablespoons brown sugar
2 tablespoons salad oil

Mix ingredients. Bring to boiling. Serve hot. Makes about 1½ cups.

Horseradish Cream

Combine 1 cup dairy sour cream, 3 tablespoons drained prepared horseradish, ¼ teaspoon salt, and dash paprika. Chill.

Dessert Pancakes

Prepare 1 cup packaged pancake mix, following label directions, *but using 1¼ cups milk*, 1 egg, and 1 tablespoon salad oil. Bake on griddle. Keep pancakes warm.

Just before serving, spread each with Whipped Orange Butter; roll up. Place in chafing dish; drizzle cakes with a little orange juice and sprinkle with sugar.

Offer Cinnamon Honey and additional Orange Butter. Makes 10 5-inch pancakes.

Whipped Orange Butter

¼ pound (1 stick or ½ cup) butter
1 tablespoon grated orange peel
2 tablespoons orange juice

Let butter stand at room temperature for 1 hour. With electric mixer at lowest speed, mix till large chunks smooth out. Gradually increase speed to high; whip till fluffy (8 to 10 minutes). Stir in peel and juice.

Cover till ready to use. (If made ahead, chill, but remove from refrigerator an hour before using.) Makes about ¾ cup.

Cinnamon Honey

Mix 1 cup honey with ½ teaspoon cinnamon and dash nutmeg; heat.

← Beef Fondue—everyone cooks

You spear a tenderloin cube on a long fondue fork, cook to order in hot oil. Take your choice of dipping sauces—truly gourmet fare! Try Cheese Fondue, too (see index listing).

Stout German fare

> **Wunderbar!**
>
> Hausplatte
> Cherry Torte, Black Forest Style*
> Mugs of Hot Coffee
>
> *See index listing

The savory aromas of sauerkraut and boiled beef foretell the pleasure of sitting down to this good German food. Plan on hearty appetites and leisurely dining—for this old-country cooking tastes best where an air of *Gemütlichkeit** reigns.

*That's comfortable old-time geniality!

We bring these recipes to you from New York's Lüchow's, famous for genuine German fare. The Hausplatte is for special occasions, but any one of the meats, served with Weinkraut, makes a dandy meal.

Hausplatte

Use a large oval plank or platter with a rim. Border with Potatoes Duchesse. Fill center with Weinkraut; top with these: Corned Pig's Knuckles, Boiled Beef, grilled precooked Bratwurst, and cooked Knackwurst (heat briefly in boiling water).

Baste meats with brown stock from Boiled Beef, well-flavored with Burgundy. Broil 5 to 8 minutes to brown potatoes lightly. Pass mustard, horseradish.

Corned Pig's Knuckles

Cover corned pig's knuckles (some markets will cure them for you) with fresh water, no salt. Add a small onion, cut in half, and a few peppercorns and bay leaves.

Simmer 2½ to 3 hours or till tender; remove from water. Cook 30 minutes with Weinkraut. Allow 1 knuckle per person.

Weinkraut

Grate 1 small onion; cook in ¼ cup butter till just tender. Add 2 tablespoons brown sugar and let melt. Add ½ teaspoon salt, 1 teaspoon vinegar, 1½ cups dry white wine, 1 cup chicken broth, 1 small potato, grated, and 1 quart sauerkraut, drained. Cook uncovered 30 minutes.

Then add 2 green apples, pared and diced, and cooked Corned Pig's Knuckles. Cover, simmer 30 minutes more. Drain kraut; use as base of Hausplatte. Serves 6.

Boiled Beef

Rub 4 pounds fresh lean beef short ribs with 1½ teaspoons salt; place in pot and cover with boiling water. Bring quickly back to boil; cook 10 minutes. Skim top.

Add 2 or 3 sprigs parsley, 4 peppercorns, and ½ teaspoon thyme. Cover, cook slowly 3 hours. Last half hour add 2 onions, 2 carrots, a parsnip, a turnip, and a bay leaf. Serve with kraut for a one-dish meal, *or* serve beef on Hausplatte.

For Hausplatte, lift out chunks of meat and place (without vegetables) on Weinkraut. Boil stock, reducing to rich gravy; add Burgundy (about ¼ cup) to ¾ cup stock. Spoon some over meats before broiling. Pass remainder. Makes 4 to 6 servings.

Potatoes Duchesse

4 cups hot mashed potatoes
1 tablespoon butter
2 beaten egg yolks

Combine ingredients; season; mix well. Using No. 7 or 9 star tip, pipe hot mixture around rim of Hausplatte plank; drizzle with 2 tablespoons melted butter. Broil.

Hausplatte – a Lüchow's special →

It was ordained by founder August Lüchow himself, for special guests: fat German sausages, boiled beef, pig's knuckles, weinkraut!

Russian spectacular stars

Classic from the steppes—lavish Chicken Kiev, side dishes that emphasize tang and tartness. Vary the menu with other Russian favorites—caviar for the appetizer, Beef Stroganoff as mainliner (see index).

> ### Gourmet's Choice
>
> Borsch
> Chicken Kiev
> Mushroom Sauce   Lemon Wedges
> French-fried Potatoes
> Cucumbers in Sour Cream
> Black-bread Sandwiches
> Prune-Cream Cheese Pastries
> Hot Tea (*in sturdy tumblers!*)

Borsch

Add 2 cups shredded beets and 1 cup *each* chopped carrots and chopped onions to 3½ cups boiling salted water; cook 20 minutes. Add 1 can beef broth, 1 cup shredded cabbage, 1 tablespoon butter; cook uncovered 15 minutes. Add 1 tablespoon lemon juice; pour into 6 bowls. Float dollops of sour cream.

Mushroom Sauce

3 tablespoons butter or margarine
½ pound fresh mushrooms, sliced
1 tablespoon all-purpose flour
1 teaspoon soy sauce
¾ cup light cream

Melt butter. Add mushrooms; sprinkle with flour; toss. Cook over medium heat, stirring occasionally, 8 to 10 minutes, or till tender. Add soy sauce; slowly stir in cream. Cook and stir till mixture bubbles and thickens. Season to taste.

Cucumber in Sour Cream

1 cucumber, thinly sliced
1 teaspoon salt
½ cup dairy sour cream
1 tablespoon vinegar
1 or 2 drops bottled hot pepper sauce
2 tablespoons chopped chives
1 teaspoon dill seed
Dash pepper

Sprinkle cucumber slices with salt; let stand 30 minutes. Drain. Combine remaining ingredients; pour over cucumbers. Chill about 30 minutes. Makes 4 or 5 servings.

Prune-Cream Cheese Pastries

Tangy-sweet filling in rich cheese pastry!

1 3-ounce package cream cheese, softened
½ cup soft butter
1 cup sifted all-purpose flour
¼ teaspoon salt

. . .

¾ cup chopped, cooked prunes
¼ teaspoon grated lemon peel
1 tablespoon lemon juice
¼ cup sugar
¼ cup chopped walnuts
2 tablespoons prune juice

Blend cream cheese with butter; mix in flour and salt. Form dough into ball; chill 3 to 4 hours.

Meanwhile, for filling, combine prunes with remaining ingredients; mix.

Divide chilled dough in half. Return one half to refrigerator. On lightly floured surface, roll other half to 12x9-inch rectangle. Cut into twelve 3-inch squares. Place about 1½ teaspoons prune filling in center of each square. Moisten edges and fold into triangles; seal edges with fork. Repeat with other half of dough.

Bake pastries on ungreased cooky sheet in moderate oven (375°) for about 12 minutes, or till golden. Sift confectioners' sugar over. Makes 2 dozen.

Chicken Kiev

1 Cut 4 medium chicken breasts lengthwise in half. Remove the skin and cut away the bone. Be careful not to tear the meat—each half should be all in one piece.

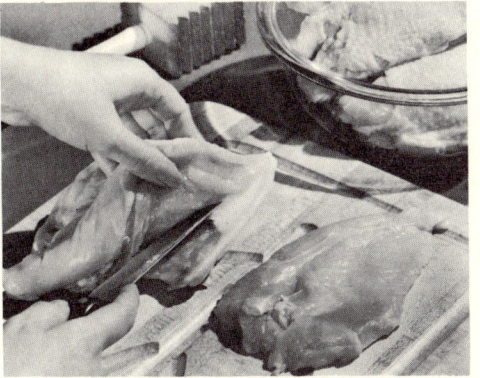

Decreed: Truly a dish fit for a czar!

The Russians are famous for Chicken Kiev, and no wonder! Under the crisp, golden coat, rich butter has melted through and through, to spurt out at the first touch of a fork.

Serve piping hot, with fluffs of parsley tucked in for trim. Complements: tart lemon wedges and creamy fresh-mushroom sauce.

2 Place each piece of chicken, boned side up, between two pieces of clear plastic wrap. Working out from center, pound with wood mallet to form cutlets not quite ¼-inch thick. Peel off wrap. Sprinkle with salt.

3 Measure 1 tablespoon *each* chopped green onion and parsley; sprinkle over cutlets. Cut a ¼-pound stick of chilled butter in 8 sticks; place a stick at end of each cutlet. Roll meat as for jellyroll, tucking in sides.

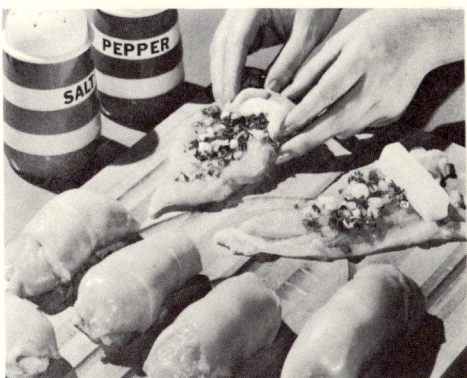

4 Press end to seal well. Dust each roll with flour and dip in beaten egg (takes 2 eggs), then roll in fine dry bread crumbs (about 1 cup). Chill thoroughly—at least 1 hour.

5 Fry chicken rolls in deep, hot fat (340°) about 5 minutes or till golden brown. Serve with mushroom sauce and pass lemon wedges if desired. Makes 4 to 6 servings.

Honorable Chinese dinner

Chinese cookery is as much an art as the carving of delicate jade.

First, the ingredients are cut up prettily (bias-sliced, diced, cut in strips), then combined in exciting ways. Crisp-cooking is the rule—to preserve bright color, fresh flavor, contrasting textures.

Result: Each dish cooks in minutes (or not at all!), looks pretty as a picture, tastes "ah so good," *and* is a breeze to eat with chopsticks, if you have the yen!

....

"Little Treasure"
(*see cover*)

Chinese Walnut Chicken
Oriental Rice
Chinese Asparagus
Sesame Cucumbers
Ginger Fruit Oriental
Almond Cookies   Green Tea

....

How to use chopsticks

Hold top chopstick like a pencil, a little above the middle, small end down. Grip *loosely* between *tips* of index and middle finger; anchor *gently* with the thumb—whole hand must be relaxed. Practice moving stick a few times to get the feel of it.

Slip lower stick into position. Rest it *lightly* on V formed by thumb and index finger and on first joint of ring finger. Don't touch lower stick with middle finger. Lower stick never moves. Try it!

Chinese Walnut Chicken

If you're planning buffet for a dozen, double the recipe. Serve in a warmer and border with rice, as shown on the cover —

- 1 cup coarsely broken walnuts
- ¼ cup salad oil
- 2 chicken breasts (raw), boned and cut lengthwise in very thin strips
- ½ teaspoon salt
- 1 cup onion slices
- 1½ cups bias-cut celery slices
- 1¼ cups chicken broth

• • •

- 1 teaspoon sugar
- 1 tablespoon cornstarch
- ¼ cup soy sauce
- 2 tablespoons cooking sherry

• • •

- 1 5-ounce can (⅔ cup) bamboo shoots, drained
- 1 5-ounce can water chestnuts, drained and sliced

In skillet, toast walnuts in hot oil, stirring constantly. Remove nuts to paper towels.

Put chicken into skillet. Sprinkle with salt. Cook, stirring frequently, 5 to 10 minutes or till tender. Remove chicken.

Put onion, celery, and ½ *cup of the* chicken broth in skillet. Cook uncovered 5 minutes or till slightly tender.

Combine sugar, cornstarch, soy sauce, and cooking sherry; add remaining chicken broth. Pour over vegetables in skillet. Cook and stir till sauce thickens.

Add chicken, bamboo shoots, water chestnuts, and walnuts. Heat through. Serve with Oriental Rice. Serves 4 to 6.

Oriental Rice

Wash 1 cup regular rice. Swish it around with hand, changing water two or three times. Drain in sieve. Put in 2-quart saucepan with 1½ cups water. Slick rice down from sides of pan. Cover and bring to vigorous boil over high heat.

Now turn heat as low as possible; cook 3 minutes. Bring back to boiling; cook 5 minutes more, gradually turning heat down. Continue to cook 15 minutes. Remove from heat. Keep pan covered; let steam 7 minutes. Fluff rice a bit (chopsticks are handy for this). Makes 3 cups.

Chinese Asparagus

Snap off woody base of stalk at "breaking point" where tender part begins. Slice on extreme bias, so slices are about ¼ inch thick and about 1½ inches long on bias.

Heat 1 tablespoon salad oil in large skillet. When hot, add 3 cups cut asparagus. Sprinkle on ½ teaspoon *each* salt and monosodium glutamate, dash pepper.

Cover; shake pan *above* high heat (like popping corn) just till tender. This takes only 4 to 5 minutes. Don't overcook!

Sesame Cucumbers

   1 tablespoon sesame seed
   1 tablespoon sugar
   ¼ teaspoon salt
   ¼ teaspoon monosodium glutamate
   1 teaspoon cornstarch
   2 tablespoons water
   ½ cup vinegar
   1 medium cucumber, unpared, sliced very thin
   1 10-ounce package frozen scallops, steamed and sliced
   ½ cup finely chopped celery

Toast sesame seeds in moderate oven (350°) about 5 minutes.

Combine next 4 ingredients. Blend in water, then vinegar. Cook and stir till mixture comes to the boil; continue cooking 1 minute. Add sesame seeds, and cool.

Sprinkle cucumbers with salt. Combine with sliced scallops and celery. Pour sesame-seed mixture over. Chill thoroughly. Makes 6 to 8 servings.

Ginger Fruit Oriental

   1 1-pound can sliced peaches, drained
   1 cup orange juice
   2 teaspoons finely chopped candied ginger
   2 bananas

Combine peach slices, orange juice, and candied ginger. Chill several hours to blend flavors.

Peel bananas and run fork down sides to flute. Slice on bias. Add to peach mixture. Heap in serving dishes. To match picture, trim with kumquats, sprigs of green leaves.

Ginger Fruit Oriental, Chinese Almond Cookies, and tiny cups of green tea are the fitting finale to this wonderful dinner.

Chinese Almond Cookies

   2¾ cups sifted all-purpose flour
   1 cup sugar
   ½ teaspoon soda
   ½ teaspoon salt
   1 cup butter, margarine, or lard
   1 slightly beaten egg
   1 teaspoon almond extract
   ⅓ cup whole blanched almonds, halved

Sift dry ingredients together into bowl. Cut in butter till mixture resembles corn meal. Add egg and almond extract; mix well. Gather up with fingers; form into ball.

Roll to slightly less than ¼ inch; cut with 2-inch round cutter. Place on ungreased cooky sheet about 2 inches apart (or form in 1-inch balls; flatten on cooky sheet with bottom of floured tumbler). Place an almond half atop each cooky. Bake at 325° for 15 to 20 minutes. Makes 50.

Atmosphere is half the fun!

Do offer your guests chopsticks (at least invite them to *try* before you bring on the forks!)—see directions, opposite page.

For fun, use a Chinese-red tablecloth, with shocking-pink or gold napkins, an arrangement of lacy spider mums, candles. Last, most exotic, touch—light incense!

Here's a sampler of our international favorites. From the sunny shores of the Mediterranean—Italian Fish Stew (Cioppino); smörgåsbord inspiration—Swedish Meat Balls and Brown Beans; exotic Indian offering—Chicken Curry, condiments

Italy

Sweden

Around the world— à la carte!

India

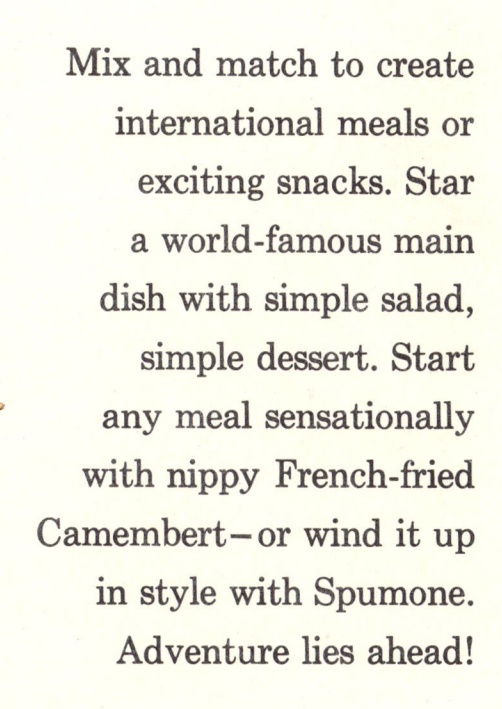

Mix and match to create international meals or exciting snacks. Star a world-famous main dish with simple salad, simple dessert. Start any meal sensationally with nippy French-fried Camembert—or wind it up in style with Spumone. Adventure lies ahead!

Appetizers and snacks

Mexican Guacamole

2 ripe, medium avocados
2½ tablespoons lemon juice
¼ teaspoon crushed garlic
2 tablespoons grated onion
½ teaspoon salt
¼ teaspoon fresh-ground pepper
2 to 4 tablespoons chopped
   canned green chilis

Sieve avocado or use electric blender. To 1 cup avocado, add remaining ingredients; blend well. Chill. To match frontispiece, trim with bacon curls. Makes 1¼ cups.

Tostadas: Start with fresh, frozen, or canned tortillas. (If frozen, thaw.) Cut each in quarters. Fry in shallow hot fat, turning once, about 4 minutes. Drain.

French Onion Soup
(Soupe à l'Oignon)

It's after-theater tradition in Paris to make a predawn stop at Les Halles, the bustling wholesale market, for a steaming bowlful of this cheese-blanketed soup. Superb!

4 large onions, sliced thin
2 tablespoons butter
2 cans condensed beef broth
1 soup can water
1 teaspoon Worcestershire sauce
   . . .
8 to 12 slices from tiny French
   loaf (or hard rolls), toasted
4 to 6 ¼-inch-thick slices Swiss
   or Parmesan cheese

Cook onions in butter till tender but not brown. Add broth, water, and Worcestershire. Cover; simmer 20 minutes. Season with salt and pepper.

Pour soup into ovenproof bowls *to nearly fill*. Float two slices toasted bread atop each. Cover each bowl with a thick slice of cheese. Place on foil (to catch cheese drips); broil 4 inches from heat just till cheese starts to melt and turn golden on edges, about 4 minutes. Serves 4 to 6.

Japanese Custard Soup
(Chawan-Mushi)

8 raw shrimp, peeled and deveined
8 spinach leaves, cut in
   1½-inch pieces
½ cup sliced fresh mushrooms
8 water chestnuts, sliced
2 slightly beaten eggs
2 cups canned chicken broth
½ teaspoon salt

Make small slit in each shrimp; pull tail through. Wilt spinach in hot water, drain. In each of eight 5-ounce custard cups (or Chawan-Mushi cups), place shrimp, spinach, mushrooms, and water chestnuts.

Combine eggs, chicken broth, and salt; pour into cups; cover with foil. Set cups on rack in Dutch oven; pour hot water around cups 1 inch deep; cover to steam.

Over medium heat, bring water *slowly* to simmering; reduce heat and cook 7 minutes or till knife inserted off center comes out clean. Top each custard with ¼ teaspoon soy sauce and a twist of lemon peel.

Island Teriyaki

Street hawkers cook it over the coals—

½ cup soy sauce
¼ cup salad oil
2 tablespoons molasses
2 teaspoons ground ginger *or*
   2 tablespoons grated gingerroot
2 teaspoons dry mustard
6 cloves garlic, minced
1½ pounds ¼-inch-thick round steak
¾ teaspoon instant meat tenderizer

Combine first 6 ingredients. Cut meat across grain in strips 1 inch wide. Use tenderizer according to label directions. Add meat to soy marinade, stirring to coat; let stand 15 minutes at room temperature. Lace strips accordion-style on skewers.

Broil 5 inches from heat 5 to 7 minutes or till cooked rare to medium-rare, turning frequently and basting with soy marinade. Serve hot as an appetizer.

Appetizers and snacks

Po Po

Let guests cook these tiny meat balls over a miniature hibachi, while you put final touches on a Hawaiian meal —

    ½ pound ground beef
    ½ teaspoon salt
    1 teaspoon monosodium glutamate
    ½ teaspoon Javanese sate spice
      or a mixture of chili powder and dry mustard
    ½ teaspoon chopped or dried rosemary
    1 egg yolk
    Grated Parmesan cheese

Mix the first 6 ingredients lightly. Form mixture into balls the size of marbles. Saute lightly in butter and roll in Parmesan cheese. Insert split bamboo stick or long toothpick in each.

Toast before eating, over charcoal in miniature hibachi. Makes about 3 dozen.

French Cheese Pastries
(Pâte Feuilleté au Fromage)

In France, this may be multi layers of flaky puff pastry, creamy cheese souffle filling. Ours is simpler, still "excellent"!—

    2 cups sifted all-purpose flour
    1 teaspoon salt
    ¾ cup shortening
    5 to 7 tablespoons cold water

    . . .

    3 tablespoons butter or margarine
    ¼ cup all-purpose flour (unsifted)
    ¼ teaspoon salt
    1 cup milk
    1 cup shredded sharp process cheese
    ½ cup shredded Parmesan cheese

Make plain pastry of first four ingredients. Make thick white sauce of next 4 ingredients, add shredded process cheese and stir till melted; set aside.

Cut pastry in half; roll each half to an 11½x7½-inch rectangle, a little less than ¼ inch thick. Line bottom of 11½x7½x1½-inch baking dish with one piece of pastry. Spread the cheese sauce over it. Top with remaining pastry. Sprinkle with Parmesan cheese.

Bake at 450° till pastry is golden, about 20 minutes. Cut in rectangles and serve hot. You'll need forks! Makes 12 servings.

French-fried Camembert
(Camembert Frit)

These nippy little tidbits – a Belgian-French import – are elegant with chilled fruit —

Cut six 1⅓-ounce triangles of Camembert* in half lengthwise, then crosswise (24 pieces). Shape crust around soft center so it covers as much of center as possible. Dip in beaten egg, then in fine dry bread crumbs, then again in egg and crumbs. (A thick coat of crumbs prevents the cheese from leaking through.)

Fry in deep hot fat (375°) till crumbs are crisp and golden brown. Drain and serve hot on small plates. Offer picks or forks.

*Or use Port du Salut. Cut in bite-size pieces or cut with melon-ball cutter; mold into small balls. Coat and fry.

Swiss Onion Cake
(Zwiebelkuchen)

    1½ cups sifted all-purpose flour
    1 teaspoon sugar
    ½ teaspoon salt
    ½ cup butter or margarine
    3 tablespoons milk

    . . .

    6 slices bacon, cut in ¼-inch strips
    3 cups chopped onion (3 medium)
    2 beaten eggs
    1 beaten egg yolk
    ¾ cup dairy sour cream
    1 tablespoon all-purpose flour
    ½ teaspoon salt
    Dash pepper
    1 teaspoon chopped chives

Sift dry ingredients into bowl; cut in butter. Add milk a tablespoon at a time, tossing just till flour is dampened. Gather into ball. Pat ⅔ of dough in bottom of 8x1½-inch round cake pan. Bake at 425° till lightly browned, about 15 minutes. Cool on rack. Turn oven down to 325°.

Fry bacon till crisp; drain. Cook onion in part of bacon fat till tender. Combine remaining ingredients, bacon, and onion.

Pat remaining dough around edge of cooled pan. Pour filling into crust. Bake at 325° till almost set, about 20 minutes. Let stand 10 minutes. Cut in wedges and serve as an appetizer. Makes 10 to 12 servings.

Meats and main dishes

Chinese Beef Skillet

Cooking takes just a few minutes. But do have the ingredients assembled ahead so there's no waiting once you start—

    1 7-ounce package frozen Chinese pea pods

    • • •

    2 tablespoons salad oil
    1 pound beef tenderloin tip, sliced paper-thin (across the grain)
    1 tablespoon salad oil
    ¼ cup chopped onion
    1 small clove garlic, minced
    4 cups thinly sliced raw cauliflowerets (1 medium head)
    1 cup canned condensed beef broth
    2 tablespoons cornstarch
    ¼ cup soy sauce
    ½ cup cold water

    • • •

    Hot cooked rice

Pour boiling water over *frozen* pea pods and carefully break apart with fork; drain immediately. Preheat electric skillet to about 410°; add 2 tablespoons salad oil. Add *half* the beef and cook briskly, turning it over and over 1 or 2 minutes or just till browned. Remove meat at once. Let skillet heat about 1 minute and repeat with remaining beef. Remove beef.

To skillet add 1 tablespoon oil, and cook onion and garlic just a few seconds. Add cauliflower; pour broth over and cook about 3 minutes or till cauliflower is crisp-cooked, stirring gently.

Mix cornstarch, soy sauce, and water; stir into mixture in skillet. Add the beef and pea pods; cook, stirring constantly till sauce thickens. Serve with fluffy rice. Pass soy sauce. Makes 6 servings.

← **Serve pork in an Oriental style**

Sweet-Sour Pork atop fluffy rice—a savory inspiration from the Far East! Round out the meal with watermelon pickles, green tea, sliced cucumbers, and fortune cookies!

Beef Cantonese

    ¼ cup soy sauce
    ¼ cup cooking sherry
    2 tablespoons sugar
    ¼ teaspoon cinnamon
    2 pounds beef chuck, cut in ½-inch cubes

    • • •

    1½ cups water
    2 tablespoons cornstarch
    2 tablespoons cold water

    • • •

    Hot cooked rice *or* Ginger Rice (*see index listing*)

Mix soy sauce, sherry, sugar, and cinnamon. Marinate beef in soy mixture 1 hour, stirring occasionally.

Add 1½ cups water; simmer covered (*don't boil*) 1 hour or till tender. Blend cornstarch and cold water; add to meat mixture. Cook and stir till mixture thickens. Serve over rice or Ginger Rice.

Sweet-Sour Pork

Next time serve over chow-mein noodles—

    1½ pounds lean pork shoulder, cut in 2x½-inch strips
    1 No. 2 can (2½ cups) pineapple chunks
    ¼ cup brown sugar
    2 tablespoons cornstarch
    ¼ cup vinegar
    2 to 3 tablespoons soy sauce
    ½ teaspoon salt
    1 small green pepper, cut in strips
    ¼ cup *thinly* sliced onion

Brown pork in small amount hot fat. Add ½ cup water; cover and simmer (*do not boil*) till tender, about 1 hour.

Drain pineapple, reserving syrup. Combine sugar and cornstarch; add pineapple syrup, vinegar, soy sauce, and salt. Add to pork; cook and stir till gravy thickens.

Add pineapple, green pepper, and onion. Cook 2 or 3 minutes. Serve over hot fluffy rice and pass extra soy sauce. Serves 7.

Chicken Lau Laus

A Polynesian dish geared to the taste of mainlanders. Made famous by Trader Vic—

    4 ounces sliced salt pork
    3½ cups stewed chicken meat in large pieces
    2 pounds taro leaves, green part of Swiss chard, *or* Chinese green chard
    2 bunches green onions, chopped (about 1 cup)
    2 tablespoons monosodium glutamate
    2 teaspoons sugar
    ½ to 1 teaspoon pepper
    ¼ cup lemon juice
    2 teaspoons cornstarch
    1 tablespoon cold water

Saute salt pork slightly; add chicken, and saute a few minutes. Add greens, and cook together for 5 minutes; add onions and seasonings, and cook for another minute. Combine cornstarch and cold water; push chicken to one side and add cornstarch mixture; cook, stirring constantly, till sauce thickens. Add salt to taste.

Put one kitchen spoonful of the lau-lau mixture in 2 pieces of ti leaves or chard and wrap in a bundle or fold like an envelope.* Put in steamer for half an hour, then serve. Makes 5 or 6 servings.

*We cooked 1 to 2 quarts lettuce (torn in pieces) with the chicken and wrapped the lau laus in aluminum foil.

Teriyaki

    3 pounds sirloin steak, 1½ inches thick
    ⅔ cup soy sauce
    ⅔ cup water
    About ¼ cup sugar-and-water syrup*
    ¼ cup cooking sherry
    1 medium gingerroot, grated (about 3 tablespoons) *or* 3 teaspoons ground ginger
    1 small clove garlic, minced

Cut sirloin in 1½-inch cubes. Marinate about 10 minutes in sauce made by combining remaining ingredients. Thread on skewers. Broil about 7 minutes or till desired doneness. Turn and brush frequently with sauce. Heat remaining sauce; pass. Teriyaki go-with: Chinese Fried Rice.

*Combine ¼ cup *each* sugar and boiling water; cook and stir till sugar dissolves.

Shrimp Chow Mein

    1 cup *each* chopped onion, sliced celery, and chopped green pepper
    1 can condensed cream of mushroom soup
    2 teaspoons cornstarch
    ¾ cup cold water
    ¼ cup soy sauce
    2 cups cleaned cooked or canned shrimp
    1 3-ounce can (⅔ cup) broiled sliced mushrooms, drained
    1 5-ounce can (⅔ cup) water chestnuts, drained
    4 cups hot chow-mein noodles

Cook onion, celery, and green pepper in ¼ cup hot salad oil 2 minutes; add soup. Blend cornstarch, cold water, and soy sauce; gradually stir into soup mixture. Cook and stir till mixture thickens.

Cut shrimp in half lengthwise; add along with mushrooms, water chestnuts, and bean sprouts. Heat thoroughly.

Serve over chow-mein noodles. Pass soy sauce. Makes 6 to 8 servings.

Shrimp Foo Yong

    ¾ cup tiny cooked shrimp*
    1 cup bean sprouts
    1 tablespoon *each* chopped green onions, chopped bamboo shoots, and finely chopped water chestnuts
    3 fresh mushrooms, chopped
    1 teaspoon monosodium glutamate
    Salt to taste
    4 eggs
    Foo Yong Sauce

Combine all ingredients except Sauce, adding eggs last. Mix well. Heat 2 tablespoons salad oil in skillet and spoon in ⅓ cup egg mixture to form each cake.

Fry over high heat till puffed and delicately browned, turning once. Stack several cakes for each serving and pass Foo Yong Sauce. Makes 6 cakes.

*For variation, substitute chopped crab, lobster, chicken, or pork.

Foo Yong Sauce: Heat 1 cup chicken broth. Add 2 tablespoons sugar, 2 teaspoons monosodium glutamate, and ¼ teaspoon sugar. Combine 1 tablespoon cornstarch and ¼ cup cold water; add to sauce. Cook and stir till mixture thickens to consistency of gravy. Salt to taste.

Meats and main dishes 35

Japanese Sukiyaki

Few small pieces beef suet
1 pound beef tenderloin, sliced paper-thin (across the grain)
2 tablespoons sugar
1 teaspoon monosodium glutamate
½ cup soy sauce
½ cup beef stock or canned condensed beef broth
2 cups 2-inch lengths bias-cut green onions
1 cup 2-inch bias-cut celery slices
½ cup thinly sliced fresh mushrooms
1 5-ounce can (⅔ cup) water chestnuts, drained, thinly sliced
1 5-ounce can (⅔ cup) slivered or diced bamboo shoots, drained
5 cups small spinach leaves
1 1-pound can bean sprouts, drained

Just before cooking time, arrange meat and vegetables attractively on large platter or tray. Have small container of sugar, monosodium glutamate, soy sauce, and beef stock handy. For "toss-stirring" you'll want to use two tools at once—chopsticks or big spoon and fork.

Preheat large (12-inch) skillet or Oriental saucepan; add suet and rub over bottom and sides to grease; when you have about 2 tablespoons melted fat, remove suet. Add beef and cook briskly, turning it over and over, 1 or 2 minutes or just till browned. Now sprinkle meat with sugar and monosodium glutamate; pour soy sauce and beef stock over. Push meat to one side. Let soy sauce bubble.

Keeping in separate groups, add onions, celery, and mushrooms. Continue cooking and toss-stirring *each group* over high heat about 1 minute; push to one side. Keeping in separate groups, add remaining vegetables in order given. Cook and toss-stir each food just until heated through. Let guests help themselves to some of everything, including sauce. Serve with rice. Pass cruet of soy sauce. Serves 4.

Note: For more batches, leave remaining sauce in pan and add soy sauce, beef stock, and seasonings by guess.

Fun for all—a Sukiyaki party →

The hostess starts things off by cooking at table, while guests sample Chawan-Mushi. Dessert: mandarin oranges, fortune cookies.

Chicken Curry

1 tablespoon curry powder
1 tablespoon butter
1 onion, minced
2 stalks celery, diced
½ cup sliced mushrooms
1 cup diced apple
½ cup beef broth
1 cup light cream
1 cup milk
2 tablespoons cornstarch
2 tablespoons cold water
Monosodium glutamate to taste
Salt to taste
2 cups diced cooked chicken

Saute curry powder in butter until nicely browned; stir in vegetables and apple; mix thoroughly. Add beef broth; bring to boil, then stir in cream and milk; bring just to boil again.

Combine cornstarch and cold water; add, and cook, stirring constantly, till mixture thickens. Stir in chicken. Season to taste. To match picture, page 29, trim with preserved kumquats and parsley. Serve with rice. Offer condiments—watermelon pickles, chutney, salted peanuts, coconut, raisins. Makes 5 or 6 servings.

Curry of Shrimp

⅓ cup butter or margarine
½ cup chopped onion
¼ to ½ cup chopped green pepper
2 cloves garlic, minced
2 cups dairy sour cream
2 teaspoons lemon juice
2 teaspoons curry powder
¾ teaspoon salt
½ teaspoon ginger
Dash chili powder
Dash pepper
3 cups cleaned cooked or canned shrimp, split lengthwise in half (about 2 pounds in shell)

Melt butter; add onion, green pepper, garlic. Cook till tender but not brown. Stir in sour cream, lemon juice, and seasonings; add shrimp. Cook over *low* heat, stirring constantly, just till hot through. (Sauce is traditionally thin.)

Serve over hot rice or Yellow Rice. Offer condiments—coconut, chopped peanuts, raisins, chutney. Makes 6 servings.

Turkish Shish Kebab

½ cup olive oil or salad oil
¼ cup lemon juice
1 teaspoon salt
1 teaspoon marjoram
1 teaspoon thyme
1 clove garlic, minced
½ cup chopped onion
¼ cup snipped parsley
2 pounds boneless lamb, cut in 1-inch cubes
Mushroom caps
Quartered green peppers

Combine first 8 ingredients for marinade. Add lamb cubes and stir to coat. Refrigerate overnight or let stand at room temperature 2 to 3 hours, turning meat occasionally. Fill skewers, alternating meat cubes with the vegetables. (For easier skewering, dip mushrooms and green-pepper pieces first in boiling water for a minute.) Sprinkle with freshly ground pepper. Broil 5 inches from heat 8 to 10 minutes or till done, basting now and then with marinade. Serve with hot cooked rice. Serves 6 to 8.

Ground Lamb with Lemon Sauce

A Greek favorite. Go-with: Artichokes—

1 pound ground lamb
½ cup chopped onion
⅓ cup packaged precooked rice
⅓ cup milk
1 beaten egg
1 teaspoon salt
Dash pepper
½ cup snipped parsley
1 beef bouillon cube
¾ cup hot water
1 to 1½ tablespoons lemon juice
2 slightly beaten eggs

Combine lamb with next 6 ingredients. Form in 25 one-inch balls; roll in parsley. Dissolve bouillon cube in water; add meat balls. Cover and simmer (*don't boil*) 30 minutes, turning occasionally. Remove meat and make Lemon Sauce. Serve over meat balls. Makes 5 or 6 servings.

Lemon Sauce: Beat lemon juice with eggs to blend. Stir small amount bouillon (from meat balls) into egg mixture; return to hot bouillon; cook and stir till mixture thickens.

Classic kabob—so delicious that everyone invented it

The words are Turkish, but many a country in the Balkans and Near East claims the kabob. You can "invent" your own, too. Add onions, red peppers, tomatoes, eggplant, or almost anything else, to the skewer.

Turkish-style accompaniments would include dolmas (stuffed vegetables, like tomato, eggplant), and a fresh fruit platter—figs, grapes, peaches.

Russian Beef Stroganoff

1 tablespoon flour
½ teaspoon salt
1 pound beef sirloin,
 cut in ¼-inch strips
2 tablespoons butter
1 cup thinly sliced mushrooms
½ cup chopped onion
1 clove garlic, minced
2 tablespoons butter
3 tablespoons flour
1 tablespoon tomato paste
1¼ cups beef stock *or* 1 can
 condensed beef broth
1 cup dairy sour cream
2 tablespoons cooking sherry

Combine 1 tablespoon flour and salt; dredge meat in mixture. Heat blazer pan of chafing dish, or skillet, then add 2 tablespoons butter. When melted, add sirloin strips; brown quickly on all sides. Add mushroom slices, onion, and garlic; cook 3 or 4 minutes till onion is barely tender. Remove meat and mushrooms from blazer pan to plate. Add 2 tablespoons butter to pan drippings; when melted, blend in 3 tablespoons flour. Add tomato paste. Now slowly pour in cold meat stock. Cook and stir till thickened.

Return browned meat and mushrooms to blazer pan. Stir in sour cream and cooking sherry; heat briefly. Keep warm over hot water. Makes 4 or 5 servings.

Serve over parsleyed rice, hot buttered noodles, buckwheat groats, or pilaf.

French Beef with Burgundy
(Boeuf à la Bourguignonne)

6 strips bacon, cut in ½-inch pieces
3 pounds beef chuck, in 1½-inch cubes
1 large carrot, sliced
1 medium onion, sliced
3 tablespoons all-purpose flour
2 cans condensed beef broth
2 cups red Burgundy wine
1 tablespoon tomato paste
2 cloves garlic, minced
½ teaspoon thyme
1 bay leaf
1 quart (about 1 pound) mushrooms
1 pound small white onions

In Dutch oven, cook bacon crisp; remove. Brown meat in the fat; remove. In drippings, brown carrot and onion. Spoon off fat; return bacon and beef to pan. Season with 1 teaspoon salt and ¼ teaspoon pepper; stir in flour. Reserve ½ *cup* broth; add remainder to stew. Add wine, tomato paste and herbs. Cover; simmer 3 hours.

Quarter large mushrooms (leave small ones whole). Saute in mixture of 3 tablespoons butter and 2 tablespoons salad oil for 5 minutes; lift out. Add small onions, brown; then add reserved broth; simmer covered till tender, about 10 minutes.

Thicken stew with *beurre manie:* Cream ¼ cup flour with 2 tablespoons butter; roll into pea-size balls. Skim fat from stew, drop in balls. Stir over very low heat till thickened. Add mushrooms, onions; bring to bubbling. Serves 8 to 10.

Sauerbraten (from Lüchow's)

    3 to 3½ pounds beef round or rump
    4 bay leaves
    ½ teaspoon peppercorns
    8 whole cloves
    2 medium onions, sliced
    1 small carrot, minced
    1 stalk celery, chopped
    1½ cups red wine vinegar
    2½ cups water
    ¼ cup butter

Rub meat with 1 teaspoon salt and ½ teaspoon pepper; place in deep earthenware crock or ovenware glass bowl; add spices and vegetables. Heat vinegar and water to boiling, pour *hot* over the meat. Let cool. Cover bowl; refrigerate. Let marinate at least 48 hours, turning meat twice a day.

When ready to cook, remove meat from marinade and dry with paper towels. Melt butter in Dutch oven and brown meat all over. Strain marinade and pour over meat. Cover tightly; simmer slowly 2½ to 3 hours or till fork tender. Remove to warmed platter, slice, and keep warm. Serves 6.

Gingersnap Gravy: For 2 cups gravy, melt 2 tablespoons sugar in a skillet, stirring till brown. Gradually stir in 1½ cups hot marinade and ½ cup water.

Add ⅔ cup gingersnap crumbs (about 8 gingersnaps); cook and stir till mixture thickens. (If you like, add ½ cup dairy sour cream.) Salt gravy to taste; ladle some over Sauerbraten and pass remainder.

German Caraway Meat Balls
(Kümmel Klops)

Make meat balls: Combine 1 pound ground beef, 1 teaspoon salt, ¼ teaspoon *each* pepper and poultry seasoning, ¼ cup fine dry bread crumbs, ¼ cup milk, 1 tablespoon chopped parsley, and 1 slightly beaten egg. Mix lightly; shape in 24 1½-inch balls. Brown slowly in hot fat; turn frequently to keep round.

Add 1 can condensed beef broth, one 3-ounce can chopped mushrooms, drained, and ½ cup chopped onion. Cover; simmer 30 minutes. Blend 1 cup dairy sour cream, 1 tablespoon flour, and ½ to 1 teaspoon caraway seed; stir into meat balls. Bring to boiling, cook 5 minutes. Serve with Spaetzels or potatoes. Serves 5 or 6.

Swiss Veal Supreme
(Escalope de Veau Cordon Bleu)

    1 pound veal round, ½ inch thick
    4 thin slices boiled ham
    8 small slices Swiss cheese
    ½ cup all-purpose flour
    1 slightly beaten egg
    ¼ cup milk
    ¼ cup butter or margarine
    1 cup fine dry bread crumbs

Cut veal in 8 pieces; pound very thin, about ⅛ inch thick. Top each of 4 pieces with 1 ham slice and 2 cheese slices (trim cheese and ham to be slightly smaller than veal slices). Top with remaining veal slices and press edges together to seal. Dip in flour, then in a mixture of the egg and milk, and last in the bread crumbs.

Melt butter in 12-inch skillet. Add meat and cook, over medium heat, about 10 minutes or till golden brown, turning once.

Remove to warm platter. If desired, swish out skillet with dry white wine and splash over meat. Trim with water cress. Serves 4.

Veal Parmesan
(Vitello Parmigiano)

Tender chops with cheese and tomato sauce. Serve with green noodles or boiled potatoes—

    ¼ cup fine dry bread crumbs
    ¼ cup grated Parmesan cheese
    ½ teaspoon salt
    ½ teaspoon paprika
    Dash fresh-ground pepper
    5 ¾-inch veal loin chops
    1 beaten egg
    2 tablespoons olive or salad oil
    5 thin slices Mozzarella cheese
    • • •
    1 8-ounce can (1 cup) seasoned tomato sauce
    1 clove garlic, crushed
    1 teaspoon crushed oregano

Mix crumbs, Parmesan cheese, salt, paprika, and pepper. Dip chops in egg, then in crumb mixture. Brown on both sides in hot olive oil. Place a slice of Mozzarella cheese atop each chop. Mix tomato sauce and garlic; pour over chops; sprinkle with oregano. Cover; simmer 50 minutes or till meat is done (add a tablespoon or so of water, if needed). Makes 4 servings.

Veal Scaloppine
(Scallopine di Vitello)

Offer crunchy Italian bread sticks, toss a salad with garlic dressing. Dessert might be spumone or a cheese and fruit tray —

> 1 pound veal round, in ¼-inch slices
> 1 cup mushrooms, thinly sliced
> ½ cup olive oil
> ½ cup cooking sauterne

Cut veal in 10 to 12 pieces of similar shape and pound *very thin*, about ⅛ inch thick. Sprinkle with salt and pepper, then flour lightly. In large skillet, cook mushrooms in 2 tablespoons of the olive oil till tender, about 4 to 5 minutes. Remove mushrooms and keep warm.

Add remaining olive oil to skillet and heat. When hot, put in several pieces of the veal and brown over high heat, about 1 minute per side. Keep the cooked meat warm while browning remainder. When all meat is browned, return mushrooms and meat to pan; add cooking sauterne and cook at high heat 1 minute. Arrange meat and mushrooms on warmed platter. Scrape bottom of pan, stirring to mix pan drippings with sauterne. Pour over meat. Makes 4 servings.

Scallopine are pounded thin, floured, and cooked *quickly*, a few at a time. Add sauteed mushrooms, a splash of sauterne — delicious!

Meats and main dishes

French Veal Stew
(Blanquette de Veau)

- 2 pounds veal shoulder, cut in ¾-inch cubes
- ¼ cup all-purpose flour
- 1 teaspoon salt
- ¼ teaspoon pepper
- 2 cups hot water
- ½ cup cooking sherry
- 1 large whole onion, studded with 2 whole cloves
- 2 carrots, cut in 1-inch pieces
- 2 cloves garlic, crushed
- Bouquet Garni (tie together few sprigs parsley, stalk celery, bay leaf)
- ½ teaspoon *each* basil, thyme, and nutmeg
- 3 beaten egg yolks
- 2 tablespoons lemon juice
- 1 tablespoon cream

Roll veal in flour seasoned with the salt and pepper; brown. Add water, sherry, vegetables, garlic, Bouquet Garni, and spices. Cover; simmer 1 hour. Discard Bouquet Garni. Combine yolks, lemon juice, cream. Add some of hot mixture to yolks, blend, add to stew. Heat and stir, just to bubbling. Serve over rice. Serves 6 to 8.

Spaghettini with Green Sauce

- 8 or 10 ounces spaghettini (or capellini, fideline, or vermicelli)

. . .

- 2 tablespoons whole basil
- 2 tablespoons parsley flakes
- ¼ cup soft butter or margarine

. . .

- 1 8-ounce package cream cheese, softened
- ⅓ cup grated Parmesan cheese
- ¼ cup olive oil or salad oil
- 1 clove garlic, minced
- ½ teaspoon pepper
- ⅔ cup boiling water

Cook spaghettini in a large amount boiling salted water until just tender (*don't overcook*); drain and keep warm.

For sauce, add basil and parsley to butter. Blend in cream cheese, Parmesan cheese, olive oil, garlic, and pepper. Stir in boiling water; blend well.

Arrange hot spaghettini on warm platter and serve with the sauce. Pass additional Parmesan cheese. Serve with crisp Italian salad. Makes 6 servings.

Here's good eating from Italy—it's rich parsley-flecked Green Sauce, atop extra-fine spaghetti. Mighty tasty—

Italian Fish Stew (*Cioppino*)

¼ cup minced onion (½ medium onion)
3 cloves garlic, minced
1 tablespoon snipped parsley
¼ cup olive oil
1 No. 2½ can (3½ cups) tomatoes
2 8-ounce cans seasoned tomato sauce
1½ cups water
1 teaspoon salt
Dash pepper
½ teaspoon crushed oregano
½ teaspoon marjoram
½ cup cooking sherry

• • •

2 ¾-pound uncooked rock-lobster tails, cut in serving pieces, shell and all
1½ pounds white fish (such as sole, haddock, halibut, cod), cut up
⅔ pound raw cleaned shrimp (1 pound in shell)
2 dozen clams in shell*, *or*
2 10½-ounce cans clams

In Dutch oven, cook onion, garlic, and parsley in hot oil, till onion is tender but not brown. Add tomatoes, tomato sauce, water, and seasonings. Cover; bring to boiling. Reduce heat; simmer uncovered ½ hour, adding sherry last 10 minutes. (Sauce may be made the day before.) Add fish and sea food to hot sauce, adding clams last; cover tightly, bring to boil, cook over very low heat for 15 minutes. (Clam shells will pop open during cooking.) Serve in heated soup bowls. Makes 6 servings.

**To prepare clams in shell:* Scrub shells. Allow clams to stand in cold salted water (⅓ cup salt to 1 gallon water) 15 to 20 minutes. Repeat twice. Store in refrigerator till ready to use.

Cannelloni

Prepare and cook Cannelloni Noodles. Place rounded tablespoon Cannelloni Filling on each noodle square; roll up jellyroll style. Place in 13x9x2-inch baking dish, seam side down. Combine ¾ cup reserved meat stock from Filling with ¾ cup light cream; pour over Cannelloni. Cover with foil. Bake at 350° for 15 minutes. Uncover; top with one 6-ounce package Provolone or Mozzarella cheese. Bake 10 minutes more, or till hot through. Serves 6 (18 rolls).

Cannelloni Noodles

1 beaten egg
2 tablespoons milk
½ teaspoon salt
1 cup sifted all-purpose flour

Combine egg, milk, and salt; add flour to make a stiff dough. Roll very thin on floured surface to a 21x10½-inch rectangle; let stand 20 minutes. Cut in 3½-inch squares; let dry 2 hours.

Cook half the noodles at a time, uncovered, in boiling salted water, about 10 minutes. Skim out; drop in cold water. Drain, spread on damp towels till ready to fill.

Cannelloni Filling

If you like, double the recipe. Serve half as a tasty stew today; use half for delicious Cannelloni Filling tomorrow—

2 tablespoons butter or margarine
1 medium onion, chopped (½ cup)
1 small carrot, sliced (⅓ cup)
1 stalk celery, diced (½ cup)
1½ pounds round steak, cut in 1½-inch cubes
½ pound pork shoulder, cut in 1½-inch cubes
½ cup cooking sherry
1 can condensed beef broth
1 tablespoon tomato paste
1 teaspoon salt
½ teaspoon basil
¼ teaspoon pepper

• • •

⅓ cup light cream
½ cup grated Parmesan cheese
½ teaspoon basil
2 slightly beaten egg yolks

In Dutch oven or large skillet melt butter. Add vegetables and cook till tender but not brown. Add meat and brown lightly on all sides. Add wine. Blend beef broth, tomato paste; add to mixture. Season with salt, pepper, and ½ teaspoon basil. Cover; bake at 300° about 2½ hours or till meat is very tender. (This finishes the stew.)

To prepare filling: Strain sauce from stew; reserve for Cannelloni topping. Put all meat and vegetables through food chopper, using coarse blade. Measure 2½ cups meat mixture; add light cream, Parmesan, basil, and egg yolks; mix well.

Meats and main dishes

Swedish Meat Balls (Köttbullar)

¾ pound lean ground beef
½ pound ground veal
¼ pound ground pork
1½ cups soft bread crumbs
1 cup light cream or half-and-half
½ cup chopped onion
1 egg
¼ cup finely chopped parsley
1½ teaspoons salt
¼ teaspoon ginger
Dash *each* pepper and nutmeg

• • •

2 tablespoons all-purpose flour
¾ cup canned condensed beef broth
¼ cup cold water
½ teaspoon instant coffee

Have meats ground together twice. Soak bread in cream about 5 minutes. Cook onion in 1 tablespoon butter till tender. Combine meats, crumb mixture, egg, onion, parsley, and seasonings. Beat till fluffy (about 5 minutes at medium speed on electric mixer, plus 8 minutes by hand).

Form in 1½-inch balls. Brown in 2 tablespoons butter, shaking skillet to keep balls round. Remove.

Make gravy: Stir flour into drippings; add broth, water, and coffee. Heat and stir until thickened. Return meat balls to gravy; cover; cook *slowly* about 30 minutes, basting occasionally. Makes 3 dozen.

Tamale Pie

1 medium onion, chopped
1 small green pepper, chopped
¾ pound ground beef
2 8-ounce cans (2 cups) seasoned
   tomato sauce
1 12-ounce can (1½ cups) whole
   kernel corn, drained
½ cup chopped pitted ripe olives
1 clove garlic, minced
1 tablespoon sugar
1 teaspoon salt
2 to 3 teaspoons chili powder
1½ cups shredded process cheese

Corn-meal Topper:

¾ cup yellow corn meal
½ teaspoon salt
2 cups cold water
1 tablespoon butter

Cook onion and green pepper in 1 tablespoon hot fat till just tender. Add meat and brown lightly; spoon off excess fat. Add next 8 ingredients. Simmer 20 to 25 minutes or till thick. Add cheese; stir till melted. Pour into 10x6x1½-inch baking dish.

Make Corn-meal Topper: Stir corn meal and ½ teaspoon salt into cold water. Cook and stir till thick. Add butter; mix well. Spoon over meat mixture, making narrow stripes. Bake at 375° 40 minutes or till top is browned. Makes 6 servings.

These steps insure typical light, well-rounded Swedish Meat Balls—

The secret of fluffy meat balls the Swedish way is in the beating. We use a mixer, then a spoon to make them feather light. Form small balls—it helps to have hands wet. For easier shaping, chill mixture first.

When browning the meat balls, do only a small batch at a time. And shake the skillet often to keep them round—*very* important the first few moments meat balls are in hot skillet. Make gravy from the pan drippings.

Wonderful with cheese

Israeli Cheese Blintzes

¾ cup sifted all-purpose flour
   or ½ cup matzo meal (cake meal)
½ teaspoon salt
1 cup milk
2 slightly beaten eggs
1½ cups well-drained cottage cheese
1 slightly beaten egg
2 tablespoons sugar
½ teaspoon vanilla
Dash cinnamon

Mix flour (or meal) and salt. Combine milk and 2 eggs; gradually add to flour, beating till smooth. Pour about 2 tablespoons batter into hot lightly greased 6-inch skillet; quickly swirl pan to spread batter evenly. Cook over medium heat till golden on bottom and edges begin to pull away from side, about 2 minutes. Loosen; turn out of skillet. Repeat.

Blend together remaining ingredients for filling. Have pancakes cooked-side up; spoon filling in center of each. Overlap sides atop filling, then overlap ends.

Brown on both sides in small amount hot fat. Serve hot, topped with sour cream and cherry preserves. Serves 6 or 7 (2 each).

Swiss Cheese Fondue

Cut ¾ pound natural Swiss cheese in strips; toss with 1 tablespoon all-purpose flour. Rub a cut garlic clove over inside of fondue cooker. Pour in 1¼ cups cooking sauterne; warm till air bubbles start to rise (don't cover or boil). *Stir all the time from now on:* Add a handful of cheese. When melted, add another handful. When mixture is blended and bubbling *gently*, stir in dash *each* pepper and nutmeg and 3 tablespoons cooking sherry.

Spear a French-bread cube through crust side with a long-handled fork and dip into the melted cheese; stir till next guest is is ready to dip—this keeps fondue smooth. (If fondue becomes too thick, add a little *warmed* sauterne.) Makes 5 or 6 servings.

Polish Cheese "Pockets"
(*Pierogi*)

Another time, serve these little puffs as dessert: Fill with sweetened blueberries, blackberries, or cherries; top with melted butter and sugar—

Filling:

1 12-ounce carton cottage cheese,
   drained and sieved
2 slightly beaten egg yolks
1 tablespoon soft butter or margarine
1 tablespoon sugar
Dash salt

"*Pockets*":

2 beaten eggs
1 teaspoon salt
¼ cup milk
About 2 cups sifted
   all-purpose flour

Combine cottage cheese, egg yolks, butter, sugar, and salt. Set filling aside.

Combine eggs, salt, and milk. Add flour to make a stiff dough. Divide dough in half. On floured surface, roll each half very thin in a 16x10-inch rectangle; cut rectangle in half crosswise.

On one rectangle of dough drop rounded teaspoons of filling in rows, 2 inches apart. Place remaining dough atop. Using wooden-spoon handle, press dough together firmly between mounds of filling. Cut apart on press marks. Press edges of dough together with fork.* Fry *or* cook in boiling water and serve as directed below. Makes 32 Pierogi.

To fry: In heavy skillet, melt ⅔ cup butter or margarine; add 6 tablespoons dry bread crumbs. Fry Pierogi till golden brown, about 5 minutes per side. Serve hot, topped with cherry preserves.

To cook in boiling water: Puffs may be cooked in boiling salted water about 12 to 15 minutes or till tender. Drain, pour melted butter over, sprinkle with cinnamon and sugar, and serve hot.

*Or you may fill 4-inch *circles* of dough. Fold in half-circles, seal, and cook.

Rice, vegetables, salads

Fluffy Rice

Cooking regular rice? Here's how—

    1 cup uncooked rice
    2 cups cold water
    ½ to 1 teaspoon salt

Put rice, water, and salt in a 2-quart saucepan; cover with a tight-fitting lid. Bring to a vigorous boil; then turn heat as low as possible. Continue to cook 14 minutes. Do not stir or lift cover. Turn off heat; allow rice to steam, covered, for an additional 10 minutes. Makes 3 cups.

Indian Rice

    ¼ cup thin onion slices
    3 tablespoons slivered almonds
    2 tablespoons butter or margarine
    ¼ cup seedless raisins
    2 cups hot, cooked long-grain rice

Cook onion and almonds in butter till golden. Add raisins and heat through until they puff. Add mixture to rice; mix lightly. Serve with curry. Serves 5.

Chinese Fried Rice

    ½ cup finely diced cooked ham, chicken, or pork
    2 tablespoons salad oil
    1 3-ounce can (⅖ cup) broiled sliced mushrooms, drained
    4 cups chilled day-old cooked rice
    1 green onion, finely chopped
    2 tablespoons soy sauce

        . . .

    1 well-beaten egg

Brown meat in hot oil; add mushrooms, rice, onion, and soy sauce. Continue to fry over low heat 10 minutes, stirring frequently. Add the well-beaten egg and continue to stir-fry for another 5 minutes or until dry enough to be fluffy. Add additional soy sauce if you prefer a darker color. Makes 6 to 8 servings.

Yellow Rice

To 2 cups boiling water, add 1 teaspoon salt and 15 grains saffron. Stir in 1 cup uncooked rice. Return to boil, cover, and cook over low heat till tender, about 25 minutes. Makes 3 cups. Serve with curry.

Ginger Rice

Cook ½ cup chopped green onions 1 minute in 3 tablespoons hot salad oil. Add 2 tablespoons finely diced candied ginger and 4 cups hot cooked rice; toss lightly. Serve with Chinese meals. Serves 6 to 8.

Fresh Mushroom Sauté
(*Champignons Sautés*)

Wash 1 pint fresh mushrooms, trim off stem ends; slice through cap and stem. Melt 3 tablespoons butter in skillet; add mushrooms; sprinkle with 2 teaspoons flour; toss to coat.

Cover and cook over low heat till tender, about 8 to 10 minutes, turning occasionally. Season with salt and pepper. Makes 4 servings as accompaniment to beef or veal.

Braised Celery Hearts
(*Céleri au jus*)

    3 celery hearts
    1 can condensed chicken consomme
    1 teaspoon fresh basil *or*
        ¼ teaspoon dried whole basil

        . . .

    2 teaspoons cornstarch
    2 tablespoons cold water

Split celery hearts lengthwise in half; trim to 6-inch lengths. Place in skillet; add consomme and basil. Simmer 15 to 20 minutes. Remove to warm serving dish.

Combine cornstarch and cold water; gradually stir into consomme in skillet. Cook and stir till mixture thickens.

Pour small amount of sauce over hot celery to glaze. Sprinkle with basil and pass remaining sauce. Makes 6 servings.

From the far Pacific— Prizes from Trader Vic's Island-Oriental cuisine—Shrimp Foo Yong and Teriyaki, at back (see index); Chinese Peas and Water Chestnuts, and Chinese Fried Rice (mold in bowl).

Hungarian Spaetzels

- 2 cups sifted all-purpose flour
- 2 eggs
- 2 egg yolks
- ⅔ cup milk
- 1½ teaspoons salt
- Dash pepper
- Dash nutmeg
- 1 tablespoon minced parsley
- ¼ cup butter or margarine
- ½ cup fresh bread crumbs
- Minced parsley

Mix first 8 ingredients. Place mixture in coarse-sieved colander over large kettle of rapidly boiling salted water (2 to 3 quarts); press through colander with tumbler, greased to prevent sticking.

When all mixture has been pressed through, cook about 5 minutes, stirring occasionally. Wash under cold water; drain. Melt butter; add bread crumbs and brown lightly. Stir in Spaetzels and brown lightly over low heat, about 10 minutes. Sprinkle with minced parsley. Serve with goulash, meat balls in gravy, other saucy European meat dishes. Makes 6 servings.

Chinese Peas with Water Chestnuts

Chinese chefs have the theory that the less cooking the better vegetables taste. Try these peas, and you'll agree—

- ⅓ cup finely chopped raw pork
- 1 tablespoon peanut or salad oil
- 2 cups Chinese green peas (podded sugar peas)
- ½ cup finely sliced water chestnuts
- 1 teaspoon monosodium glutamate

. . .

- 1 cup chicken broth

. . .

- 1 tablespoon cornstarch
- 2 tablespoons cold water

Fry the meat in hot oil in preheated skillet; add the peas and chestnuts and monosodium glutamate, then add the broth. Steam, covered, over high heat about 3 minutes. Combine cornstarch and cold water; push vegetables to one side and add cornstarch mixture to broth; cook and stir till slightly thick. Add salt to taste. Makes 3 to 4 servings. Good with Teriyaki.

German potato specials

Fluffy Dumplings and crisp Pancakes — here served at Lüchow's in New York—are traditional (and delicious) with Sauerbraten and gingersnap gravy (*see index listing*).

Potato Dumplings
(Kartoffel Klösse)

6 medium (2 pounds) potatoes, pared
2 slightly beaten eggs
¾ cup flour
½ cup farina
⅛ teaspoon nutmeg
⅛ teaspoon cinnamon
½ teaspoon sugar
1 teaspoon salt

Boil potatoes; put through ricer (makes about 4½ cups); let cool. Add rest of ingredients; beat well. Roll in balls the size of golf balls. Drop into boiling salted water to cover (1 teaspoon salt to 1 quart water)*. Let simmer 20 minutes. Lift out.

Sprinkle with parsley, *or* spread tops with Crumb Mixture: Brown 2 tablespoons minced onion and 1 cup fine dry bread crumbs in ¼ cup butter. Serve Dumplings hot. Makes 6 servings.

*It's a good idea to cook first dumpling as a test; if it falls apart, beat a little more flour into remaining mixture.

Potato Pancakes
(Kartoffel Pfannkuchen)

6 medium (2 pounds) potatoes, pared
1 small onion, grated
2 tablespoons flour
4 strips bacon, crisply cooked and crumbled
2 beaten eggs
1½ teaspoons salt
Pinch of pepper and grated nutmeg
2 tablespoons chopped parsley
Butter

Cover potatoes with cold water; drain. Grate at once; drain off water that collects. Mix potatoes, onion, flour, bacon bits, eggs, and seasonings, blending well.

Heat butter (enough to be ¼ inch deep) in skillet. Just before butter turns brown, drop in ⅓ cup batter for each pancake and flatten them out.

When golden brown on one side, turn pancakes over; cook till crisp and brown on other side. Remove to paper towels and keep warm while frying remaining pancakes. Makes 6 servings or 12 pancakes.

Green Peppers, Roman Style
(*Peperoni e Pomodori*)

½ cup thinly sliced onion
2 cloves garlic, minced
¼ cup olive oil
2 cups stewed tomatoes
2 teaspoons sugar
1 teaspoon salt
Dash pepper
½ teaspoon basil
4 to 5 large green peppers, cut in strips ¾ inch wide (4 cups)

Cook onion and garlic in *1 tablespoon* of the oil till just tender; add tomatoes and seasonings. Simmer uncovered 20 minutes.

Cook peppers in remaining oil, turning often, till *crisp*-tender. Remove to warm dish; season. Pour sauce over. Serves 5 or 6.

Zucchini Florentine

6 small zucchini, cut in ¼-inch slices
2 tablespoons butter or margarine
1 cup evaporated milk
3 slightly beaten eggs
1 teaspoon salt
¼ teaspoon pepper
¼ teaspoon garlic salt

Place zucchini in 1½-quart casserole and add butter. Bake at 400° for 15 minutes, or till zucchini is just crisp-cooked.

Combine remaining ingredients and pour over zucchini. Sprinkle with paprika. Set casserole in shallow pan, filling pan to 1 inch with hot water.

Bake at 350° for 40 minutes, or till knife inserted halfway between center and edge comes out clean. Makes 6 servings.

Swedish Brown Beans
(*Bruna Bönor*)

Wash 1-pound (2¼ cups) Swedish brown beans; drain. Add 5 cups water. Cover; let stand overnight. (Or bring water and beans slowly to boiling; reduce heat and simmer 2 minutes; cover and let stand 1 hour.)

Add 3 inches stick cinnamon and 1½ teaspoons salt. Cover; simmer 1 hour or till beans start to get tender.

Add ⅓ cup brown sugar and ¼ cup vinegar. Cook uncovered, 45 minutes or till tender; stir occasionally. Add 2 tablespoons dark corn syrup. Makes 6 servings.

Russian Salad

¾ cup olive oil
¼ cup wine vinegar
1 clove garlic
¾ teaspoon salt
¼ teaspoon pepper

• • •

7 cups crisp shredded cabbage
5 cups sliced cucumber
1½ cups drained cooked or canned peas
1½ cups sliced cooked potatoes
1½ cups drained cooked or canned sliced beets
1 cup julienne strips cooked or canned ham
1 cup dairy sour cream

Make dressing: In blender, combine first 5 ingredients; blend 10 seconds. Pour over *chilled* vegetables and ham; mix. Marinate 1 hour. Before serving, add sour cream; toss. Season to taste. Serves 8 to 10.

Italian Green Salad
(*Insalata Verde*)

1 head romaine
1 bunch leaf lettuce
2 tomatoes, cut in wedges
½ cup celery slices
½ cup diced green pepper
½ cup radish slices
¼ cup sliced green onion
1 2-ounce can anchovies, chopped

• • •

3 tablespoons olive or salad oil
2 tablespoons tarragon vinegar
2 tablespoons chopped parsley
¾ teaspoon salt
Dash fresh-ground pepper
½ teaspoon whole basil

Tear greens in bite-size pieces in a bowl; arrange vegetables and anchovies over lettuce. Sprinkle with remaining ingredients. Toss lightly. Makes 6 to 8 servings.

Dutch Cucumbers
(*Komkommersla*)

Cut unpared cucumbers in *thin* slices. Sprinkle with salt, pepper, and sugar to taste. Barely cover with mixture of half vinegar and half iced water. Chill 1 hour.

Serve drained or undrained. Trim with snipped parsley and thinly sliced radishes.

Try sturdy Swedish Rye This plump loaf boasts soft crumb, glossy crust, and "just-sweet-enough" flavor—accented by the sprinkling of caraway. Perfect for smörgåsbord; good anytime.

Breads from abroad

Danish Kringle

¾ cup butter
¼ cup sifted all-purpose flour
1 package active dry yeast
1 beaten egg
¾ cup milk
3 tablespoons sugar
1 teaspoon salt
3 to 3½ cups sifted all-purpose flour
Raisin Filling
Almond Topper

Cream butter with ¼ cup flour; roll between sheets of waxed paper to 10x4-inch rectangle. Chill. Soften yeast in ¼ cup *warm* water. Mix egg, milk, sugar, salt, yeast; stir in flour for soft dough.

On floured surface, roll to 12-inch square; place chilled butter in center; overlap sides of dough atop butter. Turn dough ¼-way around; roll to 12-inch square.

Repeat folding and rolling twice more. Wrap in waxed paper. Chill 30 minutes. Roll to 24x12-inch rectangle. Cut lengthwise in 2 strips; spread each with Raisin Filling and roll as for jelly roll, starting with long side. Moisten edges; seal. Stretch each to 30-inch length without breaking. Place seam sides down on greased baking sheet, shaping as shown, opposite page. Flatten to ½ inch with rolling pin.

Add **Almond Topper:** Brush Kringles with beaten egg; sprinkle with ¼ cup sugar and ½ cup halved almonds. Cover, let rise till double, 25 minutes. Bake at 375° for 25 to 30 minutes, or till golden. Makes two.

Raisin Filling: Add 1 teaspoon ground cardamom to ¼ cup soft butter; gradually stir in 2 cups sifted confectioners' sugar. Blend in 2 tablespoons cream; add 1 cup light seedless raisins and mix.

Breads

German Stollen

1 cake compressed yeast
¼ cup lukewarm water
½ cup butter or margarine
1 cup milk, scalded
¼ cup sugar
1 teaspoon salt
¼ teaspoon ground cardamom
4¾ to 5 cups sifted all-purpose flour
1 egg
1 cup seedless raisins
½ cup currants
¼ cup chopped mixed candied fruits
2 tablespoons grated orange peel
1 tablespoon grated lemon peel
¼ cup chopped blanched almonds

Soften yeast in water. Melt butter in milk; add sugar, salt, and cardamom; cool to lukewarm. Stir in *2 cups* of the flour. Add egg; beat well. Stir in yeast, fruits, peels, nuts. Add enough remaining flour to make soft dough. Turn out on lightly floured surface. Cover; let rise 10 minutes.

Then, knead 5 to 8 minutes. Place in lightly greased bowl, turning once to grease surface. Cover; let rise till double, 1½ hours. Punch down; turn out on lightly floured surface; divide in 3 equal parts. Cover; let rest 10 minutes.

Roll each part into a 12x7-inch rectangle. Without stretching, fold long side over to within 1 inch of opposite side; seal. Place on greased baking sheets. Cover; let rise till almost double, 30 to 45 minutes. Bake at 375° for 20 to 25 minutes, or till golden brown. While warm, brush with Glaze: Mix 2 cups sifted confectioner's sugar, ¼ cup hot water, 1 teaspoon butter. Makes 3 loaves.

Danish Kringle, a special treat

Flaky butter-rich layers fold around sweet-'n-spicy raisin filling; crisp almonds toast atop!

Go continental—pass **Butter Curls:** Dip butter curler in hot water; pull lightly over *firm* (*not hard*) pound of butter, making curls ⅛ inch thick. Dip curler in hot water after each curl.

Swedish Rye

Soften 1 package active dry yeast in ½ cup *warm* water or 1 cake compressed yeast in ½ cup *lukewarm* water. Combine 2 cups sifted rye flour, ¾ cup dark molasses, ⅓ cup shortening, 2 teaspoons salt; add 2 cups boiling water; blend well. Cool to lukewarm. Add yeast. Gradually stir in 6 to 6½ cups sifted all-purpose flour to make soft dough; mix well, turn out on well-floured surface. Cover; let rest 10 minutes. Knead till smooth, 10 minutes.

Place in lightly greased bowl, turning once to grease surface. Cover; let rise till double, 1½ to 2 hours. Punch down. Cover; let rise till almost double, 30 minutes.

Turn out on lightly floured surface; divide in 3 equal parts; form balls. Cover; let rest 15 minutes. Shape in 3 round loaves; place on greased baking sheets. Cover; let rise till almost double, 1 hour. Brush loaves with slightly beaten egg. Bake at 350° for 35 to 40 minutes. Makes 3.

Wonderful breads of Rome!—

Pane Italiano in the round is elegant for buffets. Slice it thin, make it into tasty sandwiches, then restack into a loaf to serve.

Fanciful Panini All'olio will bring raves from your guests! Long kneading develops "pull-y" crust, firm texture. Eat while fresh.

Taralli, these pretty doughnut-shaped rolls flavored with anise seed, are a favorite mid-morning or afternoon snack for children.

Italian Bread (Pane Italiano)

2 packages active dry yeast *or*
  2 cakes compressed yeast
2½ cups water
1 tablespoon salt
7¼ to 7¾ cups sifted
  all-purpose flour
Yellow corn meal
1 slightly beaten egg white

In large bowl, soften active dry yeast in *warm* water or compressed yeast in *lukewarm* water. Stir in 2 *cups* of the flour; beat well. Add salt. Then stir in *about 4½ cups* of remaining flour. (Dough will be stiff.) Turn out on lightly floured surface. Cover; let rest 10 minutes. Knead *15 to 25 minutes* or till very elastic, kneading in remaining ¾ *to 1¼ cups* flour. (Longer kneading gives typical crust.) Place dough in lightly greased bowl, turning once to grease surface. Cover; let rise till double, about 1½ hours. Punch down; let rise again till double, about 1 hour. Turn out on lightly floured surface. Divide in half; form two balls. Cover; let rest 10 minutes.

Shape *Long Loaves* or *Round Loaves*. Place on greased baking sheets sprinkled with corn meal (gives crunchy bottom crust.) Add 1 tablespoon water to egg white; brush over top and sides of loaves. Cover with damp cloth, but don't let it touch dough. (Make tent by placing cloth over tall tumblers.) Let rise till double, 1 to 1½ hours. When ready to bake, place large shallow pan on lower rack of oven; fill with boiling water. (Makes crust crisper.) Bake loaves at 375° till light brown, about 20 minutes. Brush again with egg-white mixture. Bake about 20 minutes longer or till nicely browned. Cool. Makes 2 loaves.

Long Loaves: Roll each half of dough in 15x12-inch rectangle, about ¼ inch thick. Beginning at long side, roll up tightly, sealing well as you roll. Taper ends. Place each loaf diagonally, seam side down, on baking sheet prepared as in recipe. With *sharp* knife, make diagonal cuts 2½ inches apart (⅛ to ¼ inch deep).

Round Loaves: Place the two balls of dough on large baking sheet prepared as above. With *sharp* knife score loaves, making 4 shallow cuts, 1 inch apart, across top, then making 4 crosswise cuts.

Oil Rolls (Panini All'olio)

Make these light, pretty rolls with olive oil and malt—you'll feel you're in Rome!—

- 1 package active dry yeast
  or 1 cake compressed yeast
- 1 cup water
- 2 tablespoons sugar *or* baker's malt
- 1½ teaspoons salt
- ¼ cup olive oil or salad oil
- 3¼ to 3½ cups sifted all-purpose flour
- 1 slightly beaten egg

In a large mixing bowl, soften active dry yeast in *warm* water, or compressed yeast in *lukewarm* water. Add sugar, salt, and oil; stir to dissolve sugar. Gradually add *3 cups* of the flour (or enough to make a soft dough). Turn out on floured surface. Cover; let rest 10 minutes. Knead till smooth and elastic, about 8 to 10 minutes, kneading in remaining *¼ to ½ cup flour.*

Place in lightly greased bowl, turning once to grease surface. Cover; let rise in warm place till double, about 1½ to 1¾ hours. Turn out on lightly floured surface; form in ball. Cover; let rest 10 minutes.

Shape as *Double Crescents or Taralli.* Place shaped rolls about 3 inches apart on greased baking sheet. Add 1 tablespoon water to the egg; brush mixture over top and sides of the rolls. Cover with damp cloth, but don't let it touch the dough. (Make a tent by placing cloth over tall tumblers.) Let rise in warm place till double, about 45 to 60 minutes. (When ready to bake, place large shallow pan on bottom rack of oven; fill with boiling water.)

Bake in moderate oven (375°) 20 minutes or till done. Serve warm or cool. Makes 12.

Note: For a glossier crust, brush the rolls again with the egg mixture after the first 10 minutes of baking.

Double Crescents: Roll dough in 23x12-inch rectangle. Brush with melted butter. Cut in half lengthwise to make two long strips. Cut one strip in 12 triangles, 3½ inches at base and 6 inches on sides (A in picture, next column).

Cut remaining strip lengthwise in half; then cut crosswise in thirds (each section is almost 8x3-inches); cut each section in half diagonally. (Makes 12 right triangles.)

First roll larger triangles (A) into crescents: (Stretch if dough has shrunk.) Beginning with narrow side, roll each up loosely toward point. Place point down, 3 inches apart on greased baking sheets. Curve slightly.

Roll the right triangles (B) to make spirals: Begin with narrow side and roll each up loosely, keeping straight edge even so spirals will be larger at one end than at other. Stand spirals (B), large end up, against outer curve of crescents (A), as shown below. Lightly moisten with water the place where crescents and spirals meet so they'll stick together; lean top of spiral over crescent. Brush; let rise.

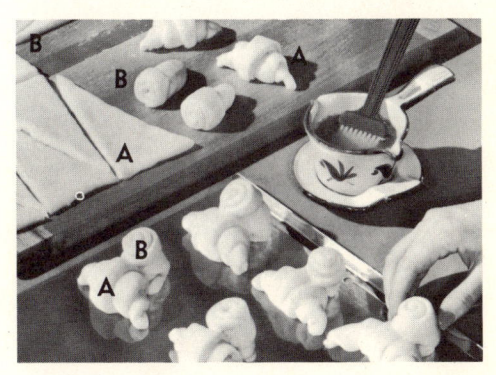

Taralli (Twists): Roll dough in 18x12-inch rectangle. Brush with melted butter; sprinkle with anise seed. Cut lengthwise in 12 strips 1½ inches wide. Holding a wooden spoon by the bowl, turn spoon while wrapping strip of dough loosely around handle. (Don't stretch dough.) Push twisted dough off handle; bring ends together to form wreath. Place 2 to 3 inches apart on greased baking sheet. Brush with egg mixture; sprinkle with additional anise seed if you like. Let rise.

Specials—Greek Anise Loaf, Lemon Buns, and Easter Basket Bread

Italian Easter Basket Bread and Lemon Buns

1 package active dry yeast *or*
   1 cake compressed yeast
¼ cup water
¾ cup milk, scalded
1 package lemon pudding
¼ cup butter or margarine
½ teaspoon salt
4 to 4½ cups sifted all-purpose flour
3 beaten eggs
8 uncooked eggs with white shells
1 beaten egg
1 tablespoon water

Soften active dry yeast in *warm* water or compressed yeast in *lukewarm* water. Pour hot milk over pudding mix, butter, and salt. Stir till butter melts and pudding dissolves; cool to lukewarm. Add 1½ *cups of the flour* and mix well. Stir in softened yeast and 3 beaten eggs; beat well. Gradually add remaining flour (or a little more or less to make a soft dough). Turn out on lightly floured surface. Cover and let rest 10 minutes.

Knead till smooth and elastic (8 to 10 minutes). Place in lightly greased bowl, turning once to grease surface. Cover; let rise till double (about 1¼ hours).

Punch down; let rise again till almost double (45 to 60 minutes). Turn out on lightly floured surface and divide dough in fourths; form in balls. Cover and let rest 10 minutes.

Easter Basket Bread: Shape 3 parts into strands, each 20 inches long; braid. Fit braid into greased 9x1½-inch round pan. (Dough will almost fill pan.) Tuck 4 uncooked eggs into braid.

Lemon Buns: Divide remaining piece of dough in 5 parts. Shape 4 parts in round buns and place on greased baking sheet. Press an egg in center of each. Divide remaining dough in 4 equal parts. Roll each in pencil-like strip, 16 inches long. Cut in 4-inch strips. Crisscross 2 strips over each egg in *buns* and *basket*, pressing ends gently into dough.

Cover and let rise till almost double (about 45 minutes). Brush all with mixture of beaten egg and water; sprinkle with decorettes. Bake at 375° for 25 to 30 minutes for Basket and 15 minutes for Buns. Makes 1 Basket and 4 Buns.

Greek Anise Loaf

1 package active dry yeast
¼ cup warm water
½ cup milk, scalded
⅓ cup cup sugar
¼ cup butter
½ teaspoon salt
¼ teaspoon oil of anise
6 drops oil of cinnamon
About 3 cups sifted all-purpose flour
1 egg

Soften yeast in water. Pour hot milk over sugar, butter, and salt; stir till butter melts. Cool to lukewarm. Stir in flavorings. Add *1 cup of the flour;* mix well. Stir in egg, softened yeast; beat well. Add remaining flour (or enough to make a soft dough). Turn out on lightly floured surface. Cover; let rest 10 minutes.

Knead till smooth and elastic (8 to 10 minutes). Place in lightly greased bowl, turning once to grease surface. Cover; let rise till double (about 1¼ hours).

Punch down. Let rise again till almost double (about 1 hour). Turn out on lightly floured surface and divide dough in thirds; form in balls. Cover; let rest 10 minutes.

Roll each part under hands to form a strand 16 inches long, tapering ends. Line up, 1 inch apart, on greased baking sheet. Braid loosely without stretching dough—beginning in middle, work toward either end. Pinch ends together. Cover; let rise till double (40 minutes).

Combine 1 slightly beaten egg and 1 tablespoon water; brush over braid; sprinkle with 2 tablespoons sesame seed. Bake at 375° for 25 minutes or till done.

Indian Puris

Cut 2 tablespoons shortening into 2 cups sifted all-purpose flour and ½ teaspoon salt. Add ½ cup shredded process cheese. Stir in enough water (½ to ⅔ cup) to make soft dough. Knead on floured surface about 10 minutes. Let rest 10 minutes.

Roll *very thin,* to 16x10 inches, on floured surface. Cut in 2½-inch circles. Fry in deep hot fat (385°) till puffed and golden, 2 to 3 minutes, turning once. (A perfect Puri resembles a fragile bubble. Discard those which don't pouf.) Drain. Serve warm with curry. Makes about 25.

To shape double-deck Brioche:

Divide dough; use ¾ to make large balls

Form the remaining ¼ into tiny topknots

Poke indentations in large balls; moisten

Add tiny balls, brush with egg white, bake

Brioche

Start these grand French rolls a day ahead—

    1 package active dry yeast *or*
        1 cake compressed yeast
    ¼ cup water
    ½ cup butter or margarine
    ⅓ cup sugar
    ½ teaspoon salt
    ½ cup milk, scalded and cooled
        to lukewarm
    3¼ cups sifted all-purpose flour
    3 beaten eggs
    1 beaten egg yolk
    1 slightly beaten egg white
    1 tablespoon sugar

Soften active dry yeast in *warm* water, compressed yeast in *lukewarm* water.

    Meanwhile, cream butter; add ⅓ cup sugar and the salt; cream thoroughly. Add lukewarm milk; stir in *1 cup* of the flour. Add softened yeast, eggs, and egg yolk; beat well. Stir in remaining flour; then beat 5 to 8 minutes longer.

    Cover; let rise till a little more than double (about 2 hours). Stir down; beat well. Cover *tightly* with foil; refrigerate overnight.

    Stir down; turn out on lightly floured surface. Divide dough in fourths. Cut 3 sections in half; form each half in 4 balls (24 in all). Form fourth section into 24 smaller balls. Place large balls in greased muffin pans. Poke indentation in top of each and moisten hole *slightly* with water. Press small ball in each indentation.

    Cover; let rise till double (about 1 hour). Combine egg white and 1 tablespoon sugar; brush tops. Bake at 375° about 15 minutes or till done. Serve warm. Makes 2 dozen.

Dramatic desserts

Savarin Chantilly

1 package active dry yeast *or*
   1 cake compressed yeast
¼ cup water
½ cup milk, scalded
⅓ cup soft butter or margarine
¼ cup sugar
½ teaspoon salt

    • • •

2 cups sifted all-purpose flour
1 egg
Savarin Syrup
Apricot Glaze
Crème Chantilly

Soften active dry yeast in *warm* water or compressed yeast in *lukewarm* water. To hot milk, add butter, sugar, and salt; stir till butter melts. Cool to lukewarm.

Stir in ½ *cup* of the flour. Beat in egg and softened yeast. Add remaining flour. Beat dough vigorously 5 to 7 minutes. Cover and let rise in warm place until double (about 1¼ hours).

Stir down batter and spoon into well-greased 6-cup ring mold. Cover; let rise till almost double (about 45 minutes).

Bake in moderate oven (350°) about 35 minutes or till done and nicely browned. Cool 5 minutes and remove from mold.

Prick top of Savarin in several places and gradually drizzle with Savarin Syrup; let stand about 30 minutes, basting frequently to soak well.

Brush entire surface with warm Apricot Glaze. Trim top with blanched almonds, candied cherries, and candied citron. At serving time, fill center with Crème Chantilly. Makes 14 servings.

Savarin Syrup: Combine 1 cup sugar and 2 cups water; bring to boiling. Remove from heat and cool to lukewarm. Stir in ½ cup kirsch, rum, or cognac.

Apricot Glaze: Heat and stir one 12-ounce jar (1¼ cups) apricot preserves; sieve.

Crème Chantilly: Whip 2 cups whipping cream with 2 tablespoons confectioners' sugar and 2 teaspoons vanilla.

Spectaculars from France   The apricot-glazed beauty is *Savarin Chantilly*, a featherlight yeast cake drenched with zingy Savarin Syrup. In front, *Mousse au Chocolat*; at right, *Crêpes Frangipane*.

Crêpes Frangipane

Fill crepes ahead; chill till time to heat—

⅛ cup sifted all-purpose flour
1 tablespoon sugar
Dash salt
1 egg
1 egg yolk
¾ cup milk
1 tablespoon butter, melted

• • •

1 recipe Almond Cream Filling
Grated unsweetened chocolate
Whipped cream

Measure first 7 ingredients into blender container or bowl; blend or beat smooth. Refrigerate several hours or till thick.

Heat heavy 6-inch skillet; grease lightly; pour in 2 tablespoons batter. Lift skillet off heat and tilt from side to side till batter covers bottom evenly. Return to heat and cook till underside of crepe is lightly browned (about 1½ minutes). To remove, invert skillet over paper towels. Repeat.

To serve: Spread about 2 tablespoons Almond Cream Filling on unbrowned side of each crepe; roll up and place folded side down in buttered 13x9x2-inch baking dish. Brush crepes with melted butter and heat at 350° for 20 to 25 minutes or till hot.

Sprinkle with grated unsweetened chocolate; sift confectioners' sugar over. Serve warm with whipped cream. Serves 5.

For fun, make Vanilla Sugar!

Split 1 or 2 vanilla beans in half; place in canister with 3 to 5 pounds sugar. Let "age" 2 weeks. Copy French chefs: Measure into whipped cream, puddings; dash over berries.

Almond Cream Filling

Mix 1 cup sugar and ¼ cup flour. Add 1 cup milk. Cook and stir till thick, then cook and stir 1 or 2 minutes longer.

Beat 2 eggs with 2 egg yolks slightly; stir some of hot mixture into eggs; return to hot mixture. While stirring, bring just to a boil, then remove from heat.

Stir in 3 tablespoons butter, 2 teaspoons vanilla, ½ teaspoon almond extract, and ½ cup ground toasted blanched almonds. Cool to room temperature. (Refrigerate if not used promptly.) Fill Crêpes.

French Chocolate Mousse
(Mousse au Chocolat)

Very elite pudding; fluffy, rich, mocha-flavored—

4 egg yolks
¾ cup sugar
¼ cup orange liqueur
1 6-ounce package (1 cup) semisweet chocolate pieces
1 teaspoon instant coffee dissolved in ¼ cup cold water
½ cup soft butter or margarine
¼ cup finely chopped candied orange peel
4 egg whites
¼ teaspoon salt
1 tablespoon sugar

In top of double boiler, beat egg yolks and ¾ cup sugar with electric or rotary beater till thick and lemon-colored. Beat in orange liqueur. Cook over *hot, not boiling* water, beating constantly, just till hot and mixture thickens slightly (about 10 minutes). Transfer top of double boiler to pan of cold water and beat till of consistency of mayonnaise, 4 or 5 minutes.

Melt chocolate over hot water; remove from heat and beat in dissolved coffee. Gradually add butter, beating smooth. Add peel; stir into egg-yolk mixture.

Beat egg whites with salt till soft peaks form; sprinkle 1 tablespoon sugar over, and beat stiff. Fold into chocolate mixture.

Pour into souffle cups, *petits pots*, or small sherbets, filling ⅔ full. Cover and chill at least 3 hours. Serve topped with whipped cream. For a Parisian touch, dot topper with crystallized violets. Serves 8.

Desserts 57

German Cherry Torte

It's cake atop and cake below, with *two* luscious fillings—butter-cream and cherry! It's rich, rich—*and* beautiful—the kind of dessert that makes European "sweets" famous!

Cherry Torte, Black Forest Style (*from Lüchow's*)

Cherry Filling:
1 1-pound can (2 cups) pitted dark
  sweet cherries
⅛ cup kirsch
1½ tablespoons cornstarch

• • •

Butter-cream:
½ pound moderately soft butter
1 1-pound package confectioners' sugar,
  sifted (about 4½ cups sifted)
3 egg yolks

• • •

2 8-inch spongecake layers,
  1 inch thick
Chocolate shot
1 1-ounce square semisweet chocolate,
  finely shaved (⅛ cup)

Filling: Drain cherries, reserving ¾ cup syrup. Halve cherries and pour kirsch over; let stand at least 2 hours. Place cornstarch in saucepan; gradually blend in reserved syrup; add cherry mixture. Heat quickly till mixture thickens and comes to boiling, stirring constantly, then cook and stir 1 minute. Cool. Chill.

Butter-cream: Beat butter and sugar together till smooth; beat in egg yolks and continue beating till light and fluffy.

Place one layer of spongecake on serving plate. From 1 cup Butter-cream, make a ½-inch border (1¼ inches high) around top of cake. Use ½ cup Butter-cream to make circle in center of cake, about 2½ inches in diameter and 1¼ inches high (same height as border).

Spread chilled cherry filling between border and center of Butter-cream. Place second cake layer on top; press down just sufficiently to make layers stick together.

Cover top and sides of both layers with remaining Butter-cream. Sprinkle sides with chocolate shot, and the top with shaved chocolate; garnish with maraschino cherries. Chill. Let stand at room temperature about 20 minutes before serving. Slice like a cake into 6 to 8 servings.

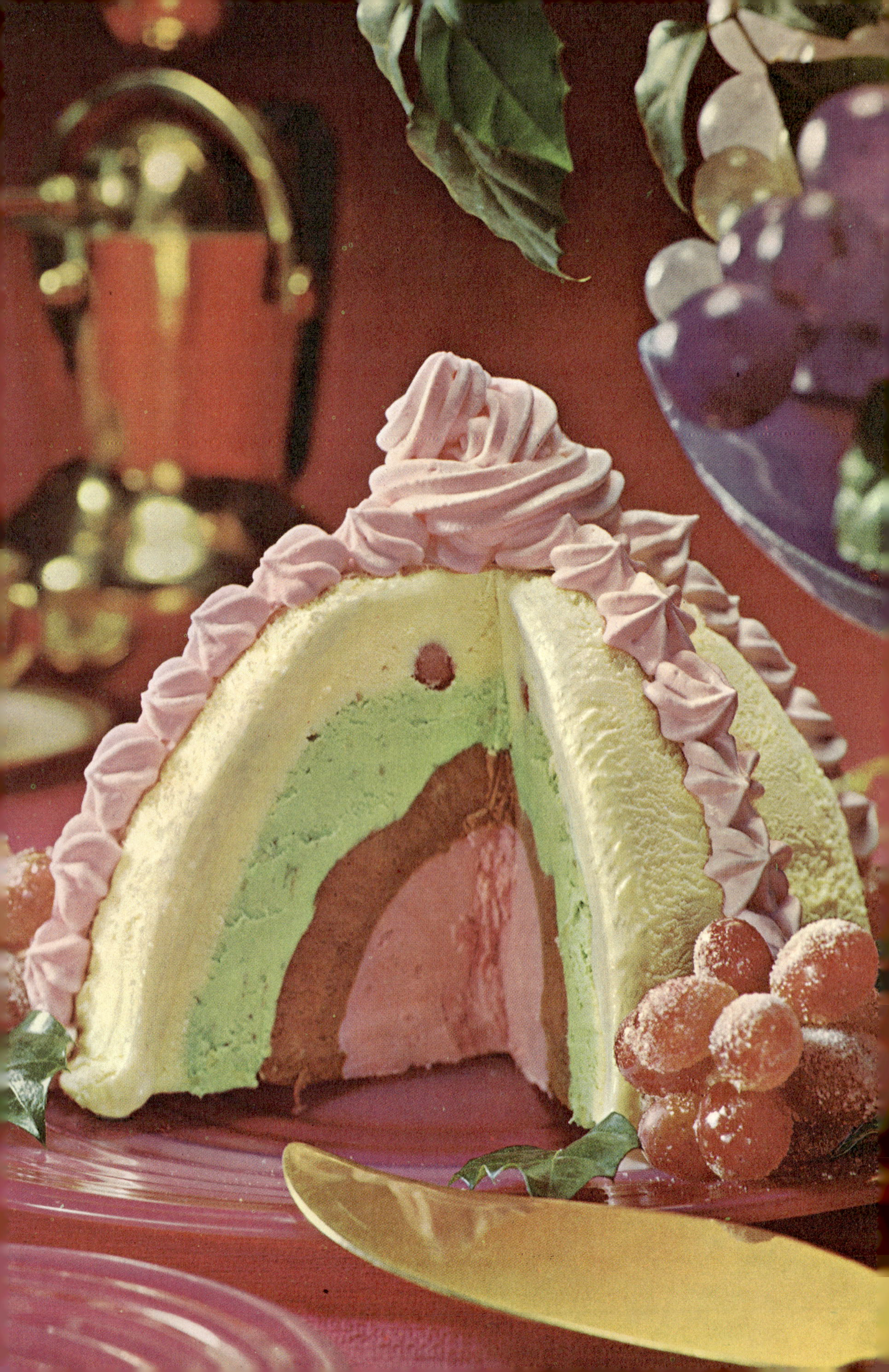

Desserts 59

Italian Spumone

1½ pints French vanilla ice cream
Rum flavoring to taste
6 candied or maraschino cherries

• • •

1½ pints French vanilla ice cream
Pistachio flavoring to taste
Few drops green food coloring
⅓ cup finely chopped unblanched almonds or pistachio nuts

• • •

¾ cup whipping cream
⅓ cup instant cocoa (dry)

• • •

1 10-ounce package frozen red raspberries, thawed
½ cup whipping cream
¼ cup sifted confectioners' sugar

Eggnog Layer: For mold, chill a 2-quart metal bowl in freezer. Stir 1½ pints ice cream just to soften; stir in rum flavoring to taste. Refreeze only till workable. With chilled spoon, spread quickly in layer over bottom and sides of *chilled* bowl, being sure ice cream comes all the way to top. (If ice cream tends to slip, refreeze in the bowl till workable.) Circle cherries around bottom of bowl. Freeze firm.

Pistachio Layer: Stir 1½ pints ice cream just to soften; stir in pistachio flavoring, green food coloring, nuts. Refreeze only till workable. Quickly spread over top and sides of first layer. Freeze firm.

Chocolate Layer: Combine ¾ cup cream and cocoa; whip to peaks. Quickly spread over Pistachio Layer. Freeze.

Raspberry Layer: Drain berries; sieve. Mix ½ cup cream, confectioners' sugar and dash salt; whip to peaks. Fold in berries. (Add a few drops red food coloring, if needed.) Pile into center of mold; smooth top. Cover with foil. Freeze 6 hours.

To serve: Peel off foil. Invert on *chilled* plate. Rub bowl with towel wrung out of hot water, to loosen; lift off bowl. Trim with pink-tinted whipped cream piped on with a pastry tube. Add frosted grapes. Cut in small wedges. Makes 12 to 16 servings.

Spumone—it's a masterpiece!—

← Trim this beauty with Frosted Grapes: Brush grape clusters with slightly beaten egg white or fruit juice; sprinkle with sugar. Let dry.

Freeze rich bombe by layers—

Stir the vanilla ice cream to soften so the outside won't melt while inside stays hard.

Working quickly, spread layers evenly. Refreeze each layer before adding next one.

Freeze firm—6 hours or overnight. Invert on *chilled* plate; loosen mold with hot towel.

Swedish Dessert Pancakes and Lingonberry Sauce

You'll think you're in Stockholm when you taste these delightful pancakes topped with the tart-sweet sauce. Keep them warm in your prettiest chafing dish, until serving time. Guests will rave about the wonderful flavor.

Lingonberry Sauce (*Lingonsylt*)

Chill, trim with pear slices. (page 7), serve with crisp cookies. Or offer as a meat accompaniment. Or spoon warm over Swedish pancakes —

    4 cups lingonberries
    ½ cup water
    1 cup sugar

Drain berries; wash and pick out leaves. Place berries in saucepan. Add water and bring to boiling. Add sugar; stir to dissolve. Simmer 10 minutes. Remove from heat; place saucepan in cold water; stir sauce a minute or two. Serve warm with pancakes, *or* chill for sauce. Makes 3 cups.

Swedish Pancakes (*Plättar*)

Beat 3 eggs till thick and lemon-colored. Stir in 1¼ cups milk. Sift together ¾ cup sifted all-purpose flour, 1 tablespoon sugar, and ½ teaspoon salt; add to egg mixture, mixing till smooth.

Drop small amount of batter (1 tablespoon for 3-inch cake) onto moderately hot, buttered griddle. Spread batter evenly to make thin cakes. Turn when underside is delicately browned. (Keep warm on towel-covered baking sheet in slow oven.)

Before serving, spoon melted butter over cakes and sprinkle with sugar. Pass warm Lingonberry Sauce. Makes 3½ dozen.

Desserts

Swedish Fruit Soup
(Blandad Fruktsoppa)

- 1 11-ounce package (1¾ cups) mixed dried fruits
- ½ cup golden seedless raisins
- 3 to 4 inches stick cinnamon
- 4 cups water

• • •

- 1 medium orange, unpared, cut in ¼-inch slices
- 1 No. 2 can (2¼ cups) unsweetened pineapple juice
- ½ cup currant jelly
- ¼ cup sugar
- 2 tablespoons quick-cooking tapioca
- ¼ teaspoon salt

Combine mixed dried fruits, raisins, cinnamon, and water. Bring to boiling, then simmer uncovered till fruits are tender, about 30 minutes.

Add remaining ingredients. Bring to a boil; cover, cook over low heat 15 minutes longer, stirring occasionally. Serve warm or chilled. Makes 8 to 10 servings.

English Trifle

- 1 layer sponge cake *or* ½ tube chiffon cake
- ⅓ cup raspberry preserves or currant jelly
- ⅓ to ½ cup cooking sherry
- 1 1-pound can (2 cups) apricot halves, drained
- 1 3- or 3¼-ounce package vanilla pudding
- 1 teaspoon vanilla

• • •

- ½ cup whipping cream, whipped
- ¼ cup toasted slivered blanched almonds

Slice cake in ½-inch-thick fingers; make into sandwiches, filling with preserves. Place *half*, spoke-fashion, in 1½-quart serving dish. Sprinkle on *half* the sherry. Repeat with remaining cake (alternating with bottom spokes) and sherry. Quarter the apricot halves; place atop.

Prepare pudding, following package directions, *but using 3 cups milk*. Remove from heat and stir in vanilla. While pudding is hot, pour over the dessert. Chill well.

Before serving, center with whipped cream and nuts. Makes 8 servings.

Viennese Torte, Sacher Style

- 3 1-ounce squares unsweetened chocolate
- ⅔ cup sugar
- ½ cup milk
- 1 beaten egg
- ½ cup shortening
- 1 cup sugar
- 1 teaspoon vanilla
- 2 eggs
- 2 cups sifted cake flour
- 1 teaspoon soda
- ¼ teaspoon salt
- ⅔ cup milk

• • •

- 1 12-ounce jar apricot preserves, sieved
- 1 recipe Chocolate Torte Frosting

Combine chocolate, ⅔ cup sugar, ½ cup milk, and beaten egg in saucepan. Cook and stir over low heat till chocolate melts and mixture thickens; cool. Stir shortening to soften. Gradually add 1 cup sugar, creaming till light and fluffy. Add vanilla. Add the 2 eggs, one at a time, beating well after each addition.

Sift together flour, soda, and salt. Add to creamed mixture alternately with ⅔ cup milk, beginning and ending with flour mixture; beat after each addition. Blend in chocolate mixture. Bake in 2 paper-lined 9x1½-inch round pans at 350° for 25 to 30 minutes or till done.

Cool layers thoroughly. Split each layer in two, using a thread (wrap around center of layer, crossing ends; pull).

Put cake together, spreading between each layer with sieved apricot preserves, then about 2 tablespoons frosting. Frost top and sides of cake with remaining frosting. Serve Viennese style with generous dollops of whipped cream.

Chocolate Torte Frosting

Melt two 1-ounce squares unsweetened chocolate and 3 tablespoons butter over hot water. Remove from heat. Stir in 3 cups sifted confectioners' sugar, dash salt, and 1½ teaspoons vanilla. Gradually stir in 5 to 6 tablespoons boiling water to make thin frosting. (If frosting begins to thicken, add additional boiling water.) Fill and frost Viennese Torte, as directed.

Index

By Countries

Austria, Hungary
Hungarian Spaetzels, 45
Viennese Torte, 61

China, Japan
Beef Cantonese, 33
Chinese Almond Cookies, 27
Chinese Asparagus, 27
Chinese Beef Skillet, 33
Chinese Fried Rice, 44
Chinese Peas with Water
  Chestnuts, 45
Chinese Walnut Chicken, 26
Ginger Fruit Oriental, 27
Ginger Rice, 44
How to use chopsticks, 26
Japanese Custard Soup, 30
  (*Chawan-Mushi*)
Oriental Rice, 26
Sesame Cucumbers, 27
Shrimp Chow Mein, 34
Shrimp Foo Yong, 34
Sukiyaki, 35
Sweet-Sour Pork, 33

England, Holland
Dutch Cucumbers, 47
  (*Komkommersla*)
English Trifle, 61

France
Braised Celery Hearts, 44
  (*Celeri au jus*)
Brioche, 54
Crepes Frangipane, 56
Demitasse, 13
Duckling with Orange
  Sauce, 12
  (*Caneton a l' Orange*)
Fish with Tarragon
  Butter, 12
  (*Poisson au Beurre
    d' Estragon*)
French Beef with
  Burgundy, 37
  (*Boeuf a la
    Bourguignonne*)
French Cheese Pastries, 31
  (*Pate Feuillete au Fromage*)
French Chocolate Mousse, 56
  (*Mousse au Chocolat*)
French Onion soup, 30
  (*Soupe a l' Oignon*)
French Strawberry Tart, 13
  (*Tarte aux Fraises*)
French Veal Stew, 40
  (*Blanquette de Veau*)
French-fried Camembert, 31
  (*Camembert Frit*)
Fresh Mushroom Saute, 44
  (*Champignons Sautes*)
Green Salad, 12
  (*Salade Verte*)
Salade Jardiniere, 12
Savarin Chantilly, 55

Germany
Boiled Beef, 22
Caraway Meat Balls, 38
  (*Kummel Klops*)
Cherry Torte, 57
Corned Pig's Knuckles, 22
German Stollen, 49
Hausplatte, 22
Potato Dumplings, 46
  (*Kartoffel Klosse*)
Potato Pancakes, 46
  (*Kartoffel Pfannkuchen*)
Potatoes Duchesse, 22
Sauerbraten, 38
Weinkraut, 22

Greece, Turkey
Greek Anise Loaf, 53
Ground Lamb with Lemon
  Sauce, 36
Turkish Shish Kebab, 36

India, Pakistan
Curries, 36
Indian Puris, 53
Indian Rice, 44
Yellow Rice, 44

Israel
Israeli Cheese Blintzes, 43

Italy
Antipasto, 18
Cannelloni, 41
Cappuccino, 18
Chicken Cacciatora, 16
  (*Pollo alla Cacciatora*)
Green Peppers, Roman
  Style, 47
  (*Peperoni e Pomodori*)
Hot Italian Dressing, 18
Italian breads, 50, 51, 53
Italian Fish Stew, 41
  (*Cioppino*)
Italian Green Salad, 47
  (*Insalata Verde*)
Italian Spumone, 59
Marinated Artichoke
  Hearts, 18
Spaghettini with Green
  Sauce, 40
Tutti-frutti Tortoni, 18
Veal Parmesan, 38
  (*Vitello Parmigiano*)
Veal Scaloppine, 39
  (*Scallopine di Vitello*)
Zucchini Florentine, 47

Mexico
Caramel Puddings, 14
Enchiladas, 14
Mexican Guacamole, 30
Tamale Pie, 42
Tostadas, 30

Polynesia, Hawaii
Chicken Lau Laus, 34
Island Teriyaki, 30
Po Po, 31
Teriyaki, 34

Russia, Poland
Borsch, 24
Chicken Kiev, 25
Cucumber in Sour Cream, 24
Polish Cheese "Pockets," 43
  (*Pierogi*)
Prune-Cream Cheese
  Pastries, 24
Russian Beef Stroganoff, 37
Russian Salad, 47

Spain
Gazpacho, 15
Spanish Paella, 15

Sweden, Denmark
Anchovy Stuffed Eggs, 8
Bowknots, 11
  (*Fattigmann*)
Cooky Tarts, 11
  (*Sandbakelser*)
Danish Kringle, 48
Decorated Chilled Ham, 10
Egg-and-Olive Penguins, 8
Herring Salad, 9
  (*Sillsallad*)
Lingonberry Sauce, 60
  (*Lingonsylt*)
Pickled Shrimp, 9
Red-and-white Salad, 10
Stuffed Celery, 8
Swedish Brown Beans, 47
  (*Bruna Bonor*)
Swedish Pancakes, 60
  (*Plattar*)
Swedish Fruit Soup, 61
  (*Blandad Fruktsoppa*)
Swedish Meat Balls, 42
  (*Kottbullar*)
Swedish Rye, 49

Switzerland
Beef Fondue, 19
Swiss Cheese Fondue, 43
Swiss Onion Cake, 31
  (*Zwiebelkuchen*)
Swiss Veal Supreme, 38
  (*Escalope de Veau
    Cordon Bleu*)

By Courses

Appetizers, snacks, soups, and extras
Anchovy Stuffed Eggs, 8
Borsch, 24
Butter Curls, 49
Egg-and-Olive Penguins, 8
French Cheese Pastries, 31
French Onion Soup, 30
French-fried Camembert, 31
Gazpacho, 15
Herring Salad, 9
Island Teriyaki, 30
Japanese Custard Soup, 30
Marinated Artichoke
  Hearts, 18
Mexican Guacamole, 30
Pickled Shrimp, 9
Po Po, 31
Salade Jardiniere, 12
Stuffed Celery, 8
Swiss Onion Cake, 31

Meats, main dishes
Beef Cantonese, 33
Beef Fondue, 19
Boiled Beef, 22
Cannelloni, 41
Chicken Cacciatora, 16
Chicken Kiev, 25
Chicken Lau Laus, 34
Chinese Beef Skillet, 33
Chinese Walnut Chicken, 26
Corned Pig's Knuckles, 22
Curries, 36
Decorated Chilled Ham, 10
Duckling with Orange
  Sauce, 12
Enchiladas, 14
Fish with Tarragon
  Butter, 12
French Beef with
  Burgundy, 37
French Veal Stew, 40
German Caraway
  Meat Balls, 38
Ground Lamb with Lemon
  Sauce, 36
Israeli Cheese Blintzes, 43
Italian Fish Stew, 40
Japanese Sukiyaki, 35
Polish Cheese "Pockets," 43
Russian Beef Stroganoff, 37
Sauerbraten, 38
Shrimp Chow Mein, 34
Shrimp Foo Yong, 34
Spaghettini with Green
  Sauce, 40
Spanish Paella, 15
Sweet-Sour Pork, 33
Swedish Meat Balls, 42
Swiss Cheese Fondue, 43
Swiss Veal Supreme, 38
Tamale Pie, 42
Teriyaki, 34
Turkish Shish Kebab, 36
Veal Parmesan, 38
Veal Scaloppine, 39

Vegetables, rice, pasta
Braised Celery Hearts, 44
Chinese Asparagus, 27
Chinese Fried Rice, 44
Chinese Peas with Water
  Chestnuts, 45
Fresh Mushroom Saute, 44
Green Peppers,
  Roman Style, 47
Hungarian Spaetzels, 45
Oriental Rice, 26
Potato Dumplings, 46
Potato Pancakes, 46
Potatoes Duchesse, 22
Rice fix-ups, 44
Swedish Brown Beans, 47
Weinkraut, 22
Zucchini Florentine, 47

Salads
Cucumber in Sour Cream, 24
Dutch Cucumbers, 47
Hot Italian Dressing, 18
Green salads, 12, 47
Onion-Bibb Salad, 19
Red-and-white Salad, 10
Russian Salad, 47
Sesame Cucumbers, 27

Breads
Brioche, 54
Danish Kringle, 48
German Stollen, 49
Greek Anise Loaf, 53
Indian Puris, 53
Italian breads, 50, 51, 53
Swedish Rye, 49

Desserts, Beverages
Banana-Nut Cake, 15
Cappuccino, 18
Caramel Puddings, 14
Cherry Torte, 57
Chinese Almond Cookies, 27
Crepes Frangipane, 56
Demitasse, 13
English Trifle, 61
French Chocolate Mousse, 56
French Strawberry Tart, 13
Ginger Fruit Oriental, 27
Italian Spumone, 59
Lingonberry Sauce, 60
Pancakes, 21, 60
Prune-Cream Cheese
  Pastries, 24
Savarin Chantilly, 55
Swedish cookies, 11
Swedish Fruit Soup, 61
Tutti-frutti Tortoni, 18
Vanilla Sugar, 56
Viennese Torte, 61